PUBLICATIONS OF THE DEPARTMENT OF
ROMANCE LANGUAGES
UNIVERSITY OF NORTH CAROLINA

General Editor: ALDO SCAGLIONE

Editorial Board: JUAN BAUTISTA AVALLE-ARCE, PABLO GIL CASADO, FRED M. CLARK, GEORGE BERNARD DANIEL, JANET W. DÍAZ, ALVA V. EBERSOLE, AUGUSTIN MAISSEN, EDWARD D. MONTGOMERY, FREDERICK W. VOGLER

NORTH CAROLINA STUDIES IN THE
ROMANCE LANGUAGES AND LITERATURES

ESSAYS; TEXTS, TEXTUAL STUDIES AND TRANSLATIONS; SYMPOSIA

Founder: URBAN TIGNER HOLMES

Editor: JUAN BAUTISTA AVALLE-ARCE
Associate Editor: FREDERICK W. VOGLER

Other publications of the Department:
Estudios de Hispanófila, Hispanófila, Romance Notes

Distributed by:

INTERNATIONAL SCHOLARLY BOOK SERVICE, INC.
P. O. BOX 4347
Portland, Oregon   97208
U. S. A.

NORTH CAROLINA STUDIES IN THE
ROMANCE LANGUAGES AND LITERATURES
Number 150

CHARLES D'ORLÉANS
AND THE ALLEGORICAL MODE

CHARLES D'ORLÉANS
AND THE
ALLEGORICAL MODE

BY

ANN TUKEY HARRISON

CHAPEL HILL

NORTH CAROLINA STUDIES IN THE ROMANCE
LANGUAGES AND LITERATURES
U.N.C. DEPARTMENT OF ROMANCE LANGUAGES
1975

Library of Congress Cataloging in Publication Data

Harrison, Ann Tukey, 1938-
 Charles d'Orléans and the allegorical mode.

(North Carolina studies in the Romance languages and literatures; no. 150.)

Bibliography: p. 120.

1. Charles d'Orléans, 1394-1465 — Allegory and symbolism. I. Title. II. Series.

PQ1553.C5H3   841'.2   74-22144

ISBN: 978-0-8078-9150-6

DEPÓSITO LEGAL: V. 4.597 - 1974   I. S. B. N. 84-399-2870-X
ARTES GRÁFICAS SOLER, S. A. - JÁVEA, 28 - VALENCIA (8) - 1975

To my father, Professor Harold Bradford Tukey, who always accepted appreciatively any efforts from his children.

ACKNOWLEDGEMENTS

The author wishes to acknowledge the College of Arts and Letters of Michigan State University which provided a research grant, summer 1967, at the beginning of this project. Professor Kenneth Scholberg's attentive reading of the manuscript led to several helpful changes, and the encouragement of Professor Georges J. Joyaux and Professor Juan A. Calvo was invaluable. Finally, the author wishes to thank her husband Michael who, as a theoretical physicist, was responsible for the guidance and support systems, which he provided with utmost trust and cheerful confidence.

CONTENTS

		Page
I.	GENERAL CONSIDERATIONS	13
II.	THE WORKINGS OF RHETORIC	37
III.	"MORT" IN A BILINGUAL BALLADE SERIES	60
IV.	ALLEGORY IN THE LONGER VERSE	76
V.	COURTLY METAPHOR AND ALLEGORY	96
VI.	CHARLES D'ORLÉANS AND HIS CONTEMPORARIES	103
VII.	CONCLUSION	118
	Selected Bibliography	122

I

GENERAL CONSIDERATIONS

Chronologically Charles d'Orléans writes midway between medieval and Renaissance allegory; his life span (1396-1465) occurs at an equal distance from the *Roman de la Rose* (1230, 1280) and *The Faerie Queene* (1590). The author of over 800 short poems in French and English, he made few forays into the sustained narrative, but rather exploited the *ballade, rondeau,* and *chanson,* all lyric types of a rigidly codified form, and unlike others of his contemporaries, he did not abandon formal writing in the courtly tradition, heavily dependent on the popular allegorical mode. His education rendered him familiar with the best of preceding works: under the watchful eye of a mother, herself an intellectual,[1] and the formal tutelage of Jean Gerson ("the most brilliant Doctoral candidate at the finest school in the West" when he received his degree at the age of thirty) (Goodrich, p. 37), Charles was imbued with a rich classical and contemporary learning. His life took place mainly in France and England with a brief trip to Italy in the 1450's, and he was thus exposed to all the literary, political, and social currents that would lead to the High Renaissance shortly after his death. For all these reasons, his works lend themselves to an examination of allegory, its potentialities and its failures, in the courtly lyric, during a period when the mode was at its peak.

The unusual length of his life, the prominence of his family, and the range of experiences he encountered have made Duke

---

[1] Norma Lorre Goodrich, *Charles Duke of Orleans* (New York: Macmillan, 1963), pp. 5-6.

Charles exceedingly attractive to a succession of literary biographers who have seen in him the epitome of an age and an elite.[2] Because of the meticulous daily records of his aristocratic household, it is possible to know which books he read from his childhood studies through the English exile and home again to Blois. His schooling, designed by Dr. Gerson personally, contained a rich harvest of medieval lore:

> Among the authors of these books were St. Augustine, St. Bernard, St. Anselm, Aristotle, Valerius Maximus, Sallust, Vegetius, Boethius, Seneca, Suetonius, Livy, John of Holywood, and Vincent de Beauvais. In his list Jean Gerson emphasized the Bible and Bible commentaries, the Church Fathers, works of philosophy, military strategy, Roman and French history, political science, morality, and physics. (Goodrich, p. 39)

Supplemental to this is the family library, basis for the Bibliothèque Nationale, started by King Charles V, and inherited from him by Charles' father, Louis d'Orléans.

> This collection boasted gold-illuminated copies of writers whose principal aim was not morality. Prince Charles as a young boy had access to the Grail stories, to Merlin, to King Arthur, to Lancelot, to the Life of Julius Caesar, to books on astrology and surgery, to a revision of Ovid — an Ovid-made-moral — and to another book that was to shape his private thoughts, his pattern of thinking by allegory — the celebrated *Romance of the Rose*. (Goodrich, pp. 39-40)

Furthermore, his family status and parental tastes contributed a personal acquaintance with the literary leaders of his era, such as Christine de Pisan, some of whose works influenced specific poems of Charles in form and content.[3] Education and environment, both bibliophilic and literate, combined to make Charles d'Orléans one of the most likely poets at a time when medieval

---

[2] Goodrich, *Charles*. Pierre Champion, *Charles d'Orléans* (Paris: Champion, 1923). Enid MacLeod, *Charles of Orleans* (New York: Viking, 1970).

[3] Sergio Cigada, "Christine de Pisan e la tradizione inglese delle poesie di Charles d'Orléans," *Aevum*, 32 (1958), 509-516.

artistry was mature. Yet critical opinion is generally not flattering in its descriptions of the stage when he wrote; it does not appear to be a high point, toward which years of preparation had aimed. What should have been the pinnacle does not stir the critical reader, primarily on account of three conditions: decadence, dilettantism, predominant allegory.

It would seem that the poets of the fifteenth century were never young, so often is their creation called decadent, the fossilized production of a moribund culture:

> Quand Orléans naquit le Moyen Age finissait, la Renaissance se dessinait à peine outre-monts, elle était imprévisible en deçà. Il n'y avait de poésie que rhétorique et de poètes que chez les fonctionnaires seigneuriaux.[4]

Pierre Champion is more benevolent, but casts the poet's writings in the same shadow, the shades of a falling night, compared to which the Renaissance will burst like sunlight.

> La poésie d'un Charles d'Orléans participe certes de cette culture de la fin du moyen âge, de cette convention élégante et gracieuse qui fut alors commune à toutes les nations polies: ... Mais il semble qu'en Charles d'Orléans, notre dernier trouvère, ce monde qui s'éteint ait voulu produire sa fleur la plus tendre et la plus parfumée.[5]

It is difficult to perceive any originality, vigor, or freshness in such an atmosphere, and when the critical evaluation begins from such a point, the ingenuousness of the poet can be lost. Is it not important to attempt to view the creating poet as new and, though struggling within an inheritance, engaged in a wholly earnest novel act each time he writes?

If one critical bias is the myth of decadence, another is the high-handed dismissal of the poet as dilettante. Charpier is particularly harsh in this regard, charging that the fault *(sic)* of Charles' poetry is that it is a pastime (p. 88). Whereas the Duke of Orleans is above all an amateur, real poets *"en ont fait l'essentiel*

---

[4] Jacques Charpier, *Vie et œuvres de Charles d'Orléans* (Paris: Seghers, 1958), p. 51.

[5] Pierre Champion, *Charles d'Orléans* (Paris: Champion, 1923), p. vi.

de leur vie" (p. 88). Charpier finds it difficult to approach the texts, "*sans pouvoir se défaire en le contemplant de la sournoise notion de dilettantisme,*" concluding

> Nous nous refusons, de nos jours, à mêler la poésie à ce banal épicurisme. (p. 89)

It is difficult to understand why dilettantism should by itself be so powerful as to destroy poetry.

Albert Pauphilet, beginning from the aristocratic pastime concept, suggests that it is not in itself an evil, but the results it may tend to form are less worthy.

> Mais peut-être nous montre-t-elle que la poésie, devenue un aristocratique divertissement, risquait d'attacher plus d'importance aux raffinements ingénieux de la forme qu'à l'originalité de l'inspiration.[6]

Ever since he Romantic revolution in taste, formal poetry has seemed less sympathetic, but the courtly lyric as written by Charles d'Orléans exhibits formalism typical of even his most currently favored opposite, Villon. It is not only the poet-princes of the fifteenth century who write formal poems.

Daniel Poirion carries the association further, linking inseparably social status, aristocratic attitude, and literary preference:

> Le récit, l'analyse, la description, telles sont les trois grandes formes de littérature qui semblent correspondre aux trois attitudes de l'aristocratie soucieuse d'agir, d'être ou d'avoir. A la curiosité, au bavardage, à l'énumération insatiable de la pensée moderne et vulgaire, l'esprit courtois oppose la consision, l'allusion discrète, la métaphore élaborée.[7]

Poirion does not condemn the aristocratic station as such, but he does connect it with the penchant for allegory, the third obstacle to appreciation of the poetry in this period.

---

[6] Albert Pauphilet, ed., *Poètes et romanciers du moyen âge*, Bibliothèque de la Pléiade (Paris: Gallimard, 1952), p. 1118.

[7] Daniel Poirion, *Le Poète et le prince* (Paris: Presses Universitaires de France, 1965), p. 62.

GENERAL CONSIDERATIONS

In the modern era, ever sensitized to new and striking images as the primary goal of the poet, allegorical verse seems to lack what is most intrinsic to poetry: lyricism. Charles Homer Haskins affirms that

> Such poetic heights were rarely reached in the Middle Ages, when the classical impulse was apt to lose itself in ... didacticism and allegory ... [8]

And Robert Guiette recounts the all too frequent disappointment of contemporary readers:

> Le lecteur moderne de "poèmes d'amour" compte découvrir dans chacune de ces pages lyriques les choses passionnées que des amants chantèrent à leur amante... Et que rencontret-il? Dans les deux mille chansons, rien, pour ainsi dire, que traditions et convention. [9]

For Huizinga, the penchant for allegory is both symptom and disease, typifying while corrupting all art of this period. He concludes that "imagination ... had been led into a blind alley by allegory" [10] and allegoric creation is labeled "the pastime of an exhausted mind" (p. 320). In fact, to this historian such artistic endeavors betray "mere decadence and senile decay" (p. 322), and Deschamps received praise for his mocking tone, since "only the note of raillery can still make the arid field of allegory flower again..." (p. 320). Allegory itself is not only suspect but nefarious.

In his study of Charles d'Orléans, Charles Beaufils acknowledges the allegorical prejudice frequently, and he even adopts a cajoling tone to encourage the reader through potentially tedious works:

> Telle est l'analyse de la première pièce de Charles d'Orléans; c'est celle qui paraîtra la plus fastidieuse aux ennemis du genre allégorique. L'allégorie s'y développe, en

---

[8] Charles Homer Haskins, *The Renaissance of the Twelfth Century* (1927; rpt. New York: Meridian Books, 1961), p. 165.
[9] Robert Guiette, "D'une poésie formelle en France au moyen âge," *Questions de littérature* (Gent: Romanica Gandensia, 1960), p. 9.
[10] Johan Huizinga, *The Waning of the Middle Ages* (1924; rpt. New York: Doubleday, 1949), pp. 318-19.

> effet, pendant 460 vers, sans compter ceux de la version anglaise. Et bien, de bonne foi, la lecture en est-elle pour cela insoutenable? Il y a des fadeurs, je l'accorde; mais le principal personnage de cette fiction, Beauté, n'a-t-il pas tout ce qu'il faut pour se faire accepter et même pour plaire? Je l'avoue, je trouve ce rôle bien soutenu et assez naturel, et je suis bien persuadé que si l'allégorie s'était toujours montrée sous un costume aussi convenable, elle n'eut pas tant excité de dégoût et de mépris.[11]

The mere presence of allegory is a signal to the zealous critic.

> Le premier âge des poésies de Charles d'Orléans est celui où l'allégorie joue le plus grand rôle, celui par conséquent qui donne le plus de prise à la critique. (p. 115)

And is Beaufils himself protesting too much, when he insists that *"cependant, l'avouerai-je, le genre allégorique n'a rien en soi qui me blesse..."* (p. 73).

Allegorical poets of classical antiquity fare better than their medieval descendants, at the hands of their critics. C. S. Lewis judges that "the earlier poets used allegory to explore worlds of new, subtle, and noble feeling, under the guidance of clear and masculine thought: profound realities are always visible while we read them."[12] In contrast to this usage, Champion notes typical and constant sameness in the fourteenth century poems, even those by recognized masters:

> les allégories sont identiques dans l'œuvre d'un Froissart et d'un Chaucer; les procédés et les sentiments ne sont pas au premier aspect bien différents. Un Anglais et un Français paraissent faire le même songe, évoquer des prairies et des fleurs toutes semblables, victimes du même irréel amour. (p. vi)

With this singular lack of originality or invention, allegory offends in its codification, seen as rigidity (though perhaps due to its popularity), and the falseness resulting from such systematization.

---

[11] Constant Beaufils, *Etude sur la vie et les poésies de Charles d'Orléans* (Coutances: Imp. Salettes, 1861), pp. 85-86.

[12] C. S. Lewis, *The Allegory of Love* (1936; rpt. New York: Galaxy Books, 1958), p. 252.

> Tout le mal (de l'allégorie) vient de l'abus qu'on en a fait; mais de quoi ne peut-on abuser? Son défaut au moyen âge, est d'être devenu un système et d'être tombé par là dans l'exaggération la plus ridicule, dans le goût le plus faux et le plus insupportable. Les ingénieuses combinaisons et les raffinements alambiques de la *géographie galante* du temps de Louis XIII, voilà, peut-être, ce qui lui a donné le coup de grâce. C'est cette quintessence du sentiment, ce sont ces subtilités métaphysiques de l'amour qui nous ont dégoûtés à tout jamais de l'allégorie et qui nous arment d'une fâcheuse prévention contre tout auteur qui en a revêtu le costume.
>
> (Beaufils, p. 73)

In fact, so strong is the opinion against medieval allegory that Beaufils can describe Charles d'Orléans' sole debt to Guillaume de Lorris as *"ce malencontreux goût pour l'allégorie,"* which is not an advantageous borrowing, but rather *"pour son malheur,"* and *"qui lui a fait tant de tort"* (p. 73); like an inexperienced and misguided schoolboy, the Duke of Orleans is seen to have sought fame in a manner deserving of our pardon since *"le prince n'est encore qu'à son début, et il n'est pas le dernier qui ait cru devoir se révéler comme poète en faisant un sacrifice au goût de son siècle..."* (p. 85).

The notions of decadence, dilettantism, and critical horror of allegory are firmly established literary traditions which must be set aside resolutely at the outset of any study of the poetry of Charles d'Orléans, who can then emerge as the young, dedicated poet for whom the courtly lyric was a preferred genre capable of subtlety, nuance, and restrained beauty worthy of the most serious and sensitive reader.

All of the verses by Charles d'Orléans are courtly and formal, and most of them admit a principal imagery based on allegory or something akin to it. The expression of individual emotion or unbridled passion did not evoke admiration in the medieval patron, as Alfred Jeanroy and Petit de Julleville have noted.[13] Yet these standards do not negate lyricism, but they do necessitate careful

---

[13] Alfred Jeanroy, *Les Origines de la poésie lyrique en France au moyen âge* (Paris: Champion, 1925), p. 339. Petit de Julleville, *Histoire de la langue et de la littérature française* (Paris: Colin, 1896), I, p. 378.

preparation from the reader before he may expect to participate fully in the aesthetic sphere of the poems. Robert Guiette, one of the most effective interpreters of medieval verse to the post-romantic twentieth century, is a skillful Virgil capable of guiding any reader venturing into the period, and of transforming the rigid forest of images-turned-trees into an intellectual paradise based on harmony, proportion, and light.

Guiette maintains that courtly formal verse demands a different type of reading than the contemporary reader generally expects:

> La poésie des chansons courtoises ne peut exister que sur un plan opposé à celui sur lequel se place la poésie romantique. Il faut lire ces chansons comme on lit des contrepoints, en en suivant les mouvements, les relations et les combinaisons, mais sans négliger la valeur sensible du thème et la qualité expressive des jeux et des combinaisons. Dans la chanson il faut considérer le chiffre ou la formule, mais percevoir en même temps la puissance incantatoire et la vie, sans lesquelles nous n'aurions qu'exercices d'école. (p. 18)

The analogy of music leads to a major distinction between medieval and modern poesis:

> D'autre part, de la chanson courtoise nous pourrons dire ce qu'on a dit de la musique du moyen âge: elle était conçue du point de vue de l'exécutant, non de celui de l'auditeur. Elle répandit la joie de l'action productrice. (p. 20)

The poem as pleasing to its maker is no new notion, but the insistence that this is the first purpose, and the dominant one, is crucial, however degrading it may appear to the reader whose tastes are then relegated to secondary status. The manuscripts upon which the current editions of Charles d'Orléans' poetry are based are private papers, which include poems by other authors which the Duke found pleasing or to which he chose to address a reply designed for his eyes only or perhaps those of his correspondent; this very atmosphere of privacy can make the reader feel excluded from some intimate circle of litterati whom he then labels idle dilettantes.

Though formal poetry, based on rhetoric and conventional themes on fixed subjects, is always in danger of becoming mere poetic form, Guiette cautions the reader not to assume that formal verse is primarily successful because of form.

> Ne confondons pas poésie formelle et perfection de la forme. Ne la confondons pas davantage avec le raffinement du style ni avec la préciosité. Il ne s'agit pas d'une question de tour, mais de la nature même de l'émotion poétique. Nous avons affaire à un autre phénomène. La fin que se propose la poésie formelle n'est pas d'exprimer quelque chose (un sujet), mais bien de révéler une forme dans son épanouissement (une chanson courtoise, ici). (p. 25)

The reader accustomed to focusing his attention on theme and searching for the new image must recognize that for the courtly poet *"Le thème n'est qu'un prétexte"*. (p. 15).

Of what, according to Guiette, does the formal, courtly poetic consist? Traditional matter renewed through poetic use of language.

> On ne saurait assez le répéter : si l'examen attentif de la chanson courtoise aboutit à la constatation d'une poésie formelle, c'est que s'y manifeste une pratique assez particulière de la poésie : elle implique un art et une rhétorique d'autant plus apparents que les sujets traités sont fixes, sont des lieux communs, assez peu nombreux pour que soit évitée absolument l'impression d'une matière neuve, et que tout l'attrait provienne, non comme certains la suggèrent à propos du rythme, d'une régularité de la forme ou du vers, mais d'une invention formelle tant dans l'organisation thématique que dans le chant. Se servant de matériaux traditionnels et de lieux communs, le poète donne au langage le pouvoir de se transformer en puissance de rénovation: (p. 21).

The courtly poet, writing within this structured, inherited tradition, risks repetitions which also haunt any prolific artist, as Alfred Glauser has sensitively noted.

> Quand le poète pratique longuement le même genre, il court le risque de se répéter et de se parodier lui-même. Son style devient une habitude qui conduit à une certaine paresse. Son métier s'accompagne de manies dont il ne

peut pas se défaire. Il y a des moments où, sans émotion et sans envie, il se copie lui-même, où il écrit malgré lui et hors de lui.[14]

Charles d'Orléans escapes this constant danger, producing innovative "constellations of metaphors" as one of his most illuminating critics, Sergio Cigada, has written.

> La poesie di Charles d'Orleans tuttavia, questo è ben chiaro, non consiste nelle descrizione lirica di un sentimento individuale; e non consiste neanche nel puro acquiescere al cristallizzato, ritmico gioco cortese. Charles ha accostato a questi primi due un terzo piano d'Immagini, che generano tutto un nuovo gioco di rispondenze, e nelle quali consiste la vera, seppur tenue, poesia della ballata: tutta una piccola costellazione di metafore in cui si traspone il gioco del sentimento...[15]

Just as rhetoric is central to an appreciation of the courtly lyric and its particular emphasis on form, this use of metaphor and its relation to full allegory is at the heart of the originality and innovation of Charles d'Orléans as well as being essential to any characterization of the fifteenth century courtly lyric. An evaluation of the Duke's role and expertise depends then on an understanding of allegory itself, personification, metaphor, and courtly metaphor, for which a brief review of a few studies may be a useful prelude.

In the medieval works which Charles studied, allegory is frequent in all genres of writing, and in the visual arts as well. Because of the recurrence and lack of generic restriction, the process has subsequently interested a wide range of scholars, and the term "allegory" is often defined; yet, in spite of a vague common residual meaning, the elusive nature of the word's significance is readily apparent when traversing the critical literature and finding that not only different scholars but the same author in different passages may assign allegory variant spheres of meaning in each context.

---

[14] Alfred Glauser, *Le Poème-symbole* (Paris: Nizet, 1967), p. 9.
[15] Sergio Cigada, *L'Opera poetica di Charles d'Orléans* (Milano: Società Editrice Vita e Pensiero, 1960), p. 98.

Charles d'Orléans has been called a poet of *"perpétuelle allégorie,"* by one of his most careful and admiring biographers (Champion, p. vii), and manuals of French literary history carefully preserve this convenient epithet; the generalization characterizes an intellectual procedure or point of view of assumedly recognizable nature, and serves to situate this poet generally within the medieval stream of a particular rhetorical cenvention, under the aegis of the *Roman de la Rose.* It also associates the Duke of Orleans with a poetry that may be studied and distant rather than spontaneous and immediate in its creation and its appeal. Yet such a brief and facile summary phrase is impressionistic and contributes little to any specific grasp of this poet's particular technique or that of any other artist who uses allegory very much.

Kellogg and Steele, introducing an edition of Spenser's *Faerie Queen,* focus directly and strictly on the functioning of literary allegory, which for them is "the personification of abstract ideas with mimetic detail." [16] It is a rhetorical device (personification) with a clear psychological function in terms of the author and reader (memory of abstraction, facilitated by detail). Kellogg and Steele imply that usually personification is the principal working tool, contributory to allegory, and not merely one deviant or subordinate type out of many. The mode depends upon a common set of conventional images and material. As illustrations of this, Kellogg and Steele choose Chaucer's wife of Bath, *la vieille* from the *Roman de la rose,* and the Samaritan woman from *John* 4:7-36, and maintain that in each case the woman,

> for her full significance is dependent upon the reader's familiarity with a conventional literary image and with the doctrine, attached to that image, of man's gall through permitting his passion to gain sovereignty over his reason. (p. 8)

Allegory is then an intellectual process involving three elements: the idea to be suggested or conveyed (or doctrine), the personification (or literary image) which may or may not realize a successful

---

[16] Edmund Spenser, *The Faerie Queene, I and II,* ed. Robert Kellogg and Oliver Steele (New York: Odyssey, 1965), p. 8.

rhetorical existence, and the traditional convention attached to the image.

The mechanics of allegory, or its precise rhetorical nature, are less interesting to Kellogg and Steele than this concept of allegory's tri-partite nature; furthermore, their interest follows neither the mechanism of allegory nor the poetic process of its creation, but its resultant achievements and their portative doctrinal meanings.

> Allegorical fictions do not imitate actual people and events to produce ethically typical characters and probable actions. Even when they are most mimetic allegorical fictions illustrate some further metaphysical, theological, ethical or social doctrine through the manipulation of images that have stipulated meanings *other than* their meanings as imitations of the actual world. The writer of an allegorical fiction looks back to literary tradition for images that have acquired some meaning other than mere representation of the actual world, and he looks to his intellectual and religious tradition for the ideas his fiction is to illustate. (pp. 7-8)

In that their comments preface a narrative, their concept is one of narrative allegory; perforce, relating to *The Faerie Queen* Kellogg and Steele are attentive to active characters and latent or residual ideas represented by characters in a fiction. One of the most important criteria for judging successful allegory for them will be sustained, continuous, prolonged symbolism.

> Since the eighteenth century the term allegorical has been used only for those literary works which tend to become discursive in the sense that each element of the fiction bears an unmistakeable reference to some element in a continuous argument. A better term for symbolism of this sort is "naive allegory" or "allegory of ideas." (p. 6)

What the author intends and what he actually creates may not always constitute a unity; Kellogg and Steele describe this phenomenon as allegory transformed or escaped into "something else."

> Naive allegory in a pure form is rare in literature. Only with difficulty can poets manage to create a fiction in which the characters and actions represent nothing other than elements in a coherent argument. When the charac-

ters begin to take on lives of their own, when they and
the actions they engage in are understood as imitations
of real people and events, naive allegory gives place to
something else. (p. 6)

Kellogg and Steele delimit literary narrative allegory as a fiction drawn from a tradition common to author and public which may eventually obtain a life and interest of its own apart from the argument it originally represents. Kellogg and Steele describe the function of allegory in literature, and although their definition arises from an examination of the narrative, it can be adapted to the lyric of Charles d'Orléans. In their terms, the Duke of Orleans seeks to express or evoke a mood or personal view (Kellogg and Steele's doctrine) and uses a variety of personifications, in full cognizance of a climate of conventional associations attached to the figurative language he employs. But, unlike the narrative, in the short poem, an independent existence is not necessarily the *summum bonum* for a personified abstraction; rather, a twilight or subordinated life of suggested embodiment may suit the purposes of the lyricist far better than full-bodied independence. Charles' awareness of this and his resulting constraint make him a better poet though an inferior allegorist in the narrative sense. His use of levels of allegory, a technique perhaps intolerable in a writer of narrative, is the key to his excellence as a practitioner of allegory in the short lyric.

Critical attention to allegory has moved in several divergent directions suggested by Kellogg and Steele: 1) content, represented in the following discussion by Owen; 2) psychological processes, research typified by Angus Fletcher; 3) the developmentally construed cultural synthesis of method and literary product, presented by C. S. Lewis; 4) an attempt to schematize techniques, undertaken by Arnold Williams.

Though many scholars have commented on the vastness of allegory's domain and its technical multiplicity, few have actually attempted to plot its ground specifically. Owen's work is singular in its persistently clear generalizations from the concrete, and the insistence on the greater validity of schema to be drawn from a range of selected texts, or their universal application as categories. She writes tersely:

Allegory may be used (1) to delineate contemporary life from the point of view of the reformer or of the pure satirist, as in "Gulliver's Travels"; (2) to provide instruction in sacred or secular learning as in the Morality Plays; (3) to state abstract ethical truths as in "The Faerie Queen"; (4) to embody the personal experience of the writer, (a) having a universal application as in the case of "The Pilgrim's Progress" or (b) being merely phrases and incidents, moral and material, of his career as in the account of Spenser's wooing in the "Faerie Queen," Book VI.[17]

The definiteness and neatness of the frames comes from their dependence upon specific works, as opposed to process, method, or relation to human intellect in general. The lyric production of Charles d'Orléans is certainly describable as (4) the embodiment of his personal experience (as the diligent attempts to identify the ladies of his love poetry eloquently testify). Some of his verses are indeed incidental while others aspire to universality, but as was true for Kellogg and Steele, Owen's very keen sense of narrative allegory causes some omissions or awkwardness when transferred to the short lyric.

The schema does not account for stages or levels of allegorical practice (within the same work or the same author's works), the balance between allegory, personification, and metaphor. Rhetoric, in all its diversity and fascinating complexity, is properly subdued or absent in this study of content, but for short verse linguistic or rhetorical distinctions are essential.

In the works of Charles d'Orléans, the development of a poetic, consciously dependent on allegory ever more skillfully deployed, cannot be accounted for in Owen's terms; a stanza like the following requires a different methodology or approach:

> Quant je suis couschie en mon lit
> Je ne puis en paix reposer;
> Car toute la nuit mon cueur lit

---

[17] Dorothy L. Owen, Piers Plowman: *A Comparison with Some Earlier and Contemporary French Allegories* (London: Hodder and Stoughton, 1912), p. 12.

> Ou rommant de Plaisant Penser,
> Et me prie de l'escouter; [18]
>
> (Ballade VIII, vv. 1-5)

Angus Fletcher does not devote attention to medieval or pre-Renaissance allegory, preferring like most behavioralists to draw and demonstrate his theories from later more nearly modern works. Ideas relevant to this study may be too simple: "In simplest terms, allegory says one thing and means another." [19] But his expansions of this thought reveal again the limitations of considering sustained narrative allegory to be of the same aesthetic process as the forms of allegory appropriate to the short poem, especially in the late medieval courly setting.

> (on author's intent:) ... allegorical or partly allegorical works — by which we mean primarily that as they go along they are usually saying one thing in order to mean something beyond that one thing. (p. 4)

> (on patron's perception:) *Allegoria* manifestly has two or more levels of meaning, and the apprehension of these must require at least two attitudes of mind. (p. 18)

In the short lyric, allegory as expanded metaphor may be the device employed without hope of conveying a second separate meaning. Rather the merging of two levels (what is said and what is meant) may produce a stronger image, potentially richer and more gracefully elusive at the same time. In those poems where Charles d'Orléans differentiates the two spheres of the allegorical mode least clearly, he can be the most successful.

> Rondeau CCXXXII
> Ce n'est que chose acoustumee
> Quant Soussy voy vers moy venir
> Se tost ne lui venoye ouvrir,
> Il romproit l'uis de ma Pensee.

---

[18] Charles d'Orléans, *Poésies,* ed. Pierre Champion (1923: rpt. Paris: Champion, 1966). All quotations from French poetry by Charles d'Orléans cited in this study are from the Champion edition and follow the numbering of items used by Champion.

[19] Angus Fletcher, *Allegory* (Ithaca: Cornell Univ. Press, 1964), p. 2.

> Lors fait d'escremie levee,
> Et puis vient mon cueur assaillir.
> Ce n'est que chose acoustumee
> Quant Soussy voy vers moy venir.
>
> Adonc prent d'espoir son espee,
> Mon cueur, pour dez coups soy couvrir
> Et se deffendre et garentir
> Ainsi je passe la journee
> Ce n'est que chose acoustumee.

At first glance, this uncomplicated rondeau offers precisely the two-part universe of which the reader must be aware: 1) the assault on a dwelling by an enemy against whom vigilant defense must be mounted, phenomena described in the vocabulary of the exterior world of action; 2) the mental state of the poet who fights against depression trying to be hopeful. Yet, the success of the poem stems from the merger of the two arenas, rather than from their separateness. The poet acts as bridge, and his presence is signaled by the approach of Soussy to him directly *(vers moy)*, by his act of opening the door *(venoye)*. The transfer from first person in the opening stanza to third person (*Mon cueur* receiving the brunt of the attack) creates distance, and it would seem that the real allegory has been achieved. But Charles skillfully effects a new union between himself and his heart in the penultimate line: *Ainsi je passe la journee.* It is the interplay of the two levels of meaning, and ultimately their fusion, which is important to the rhetorica of the Duke of Orleans.

For C. S. Lewis, allegory is the mode of expression corresponding to symbolism as a mode of thought. (p. 48) It is used for revealing "that which cannot be said, or so well said, in literal speech." (p. 166). It functions as the agency for recounting the reflective life in the ages before scientific consciousness of the multifaceted human psychology.

> The inner life, and specially the life of love, religion, and spiritual adventure, has therefore always been the field of true allegory; for here there are intangibles which only allegory can fix and reticences which only allegory can overcome. (p. 166)

"The life of love, religion, and spiritual adventure" — can there be a more appropriate or felicitous description of the themes and content of verse by the Duke of Orleans? Lewis also suggests three levels of allegory, in various passages of *The Allegory of Love*:

> 1. *The Compleynt unto Pite* and the *Compleynt to His Lady* illustrate the use of personification at its lowest level — the most faint and frigid result of the popularity of allegory. Not only do the allegorical figures fail to interact, as in a true allegory; they even fail to be pictorial: they become a mere catalogue: (p. 167).
> 2. He (Lydgate) uses allegory merely as a framework for effusions which are unallegorical or which, at the most, reintroduce allegory only in the form of rhetorical personifications. (p. 239)
> 3. It (Chaucer's *Parlement of Foules*) is not radical allegory, by my standard, for it allegorizes no inner action. (p. 174)

Catalogue, rhetorical personification, radical allegory are all three apparent in the works of Charles d'Orléans, though the last category is perhaps more readily applicable to the narrative than the lyric. "By a radical allegory I mean a story which can be translated into literal narrative..." (p. 166).

Lewis also notes in passing "traces of the allegorical poem" which may occur: the framework of a dream, allegory itself as a framework, allegorical persons, and personifications (p. 167). Perhaps because he has worked with late medieval works, Lewis is aware of the nuances, rhetorical and intellectual, which must be grasped to appreciate more fully the verse of Charles d'Orléans and his contemporaries. Lewis intuits the diversity and complexity of the mode which, far from being a homogeneous and simplisitically boring routine, appealed to its users because of its complication and opportunity for individuality, subtlety, and moderate invention. His thoughts, while not providing a framework for analysis, are stimulating and potentially productive.

Arnold Williams, desiring a clear schema to account for the disparateness Lewis suggests, defines three major elements of allegory from a study of selected medieval texts: "a cast of personages, a series of connected actions, and a set of signs, signals, and structures."[20] The personage is either a personation or a figuration, while personification becomes, for Williams, a stage of personation. Personation and figuration differ in their point of origin; whereas a personation (whose name indicates his nature)

> begins as a conceptual entity, some sort of abstraction, which does not correspond to any existent thing in the actual world... figurations begin as specific individuals, historical, mythological, legendary, or even fictional... (p. 79).

Personifications, personations, and figurations all exist within the verse of Charles d'Orléans, although rarely in a precise juxtaposition or contrast with each other. What is more important is the use of other kinds of person in the allegorical milieu, in addition to Williams' three (or two) personage types.

The second element of allegory, the series of connected actions, is basically plot, and therefore primarily narrative and not appropriate to the lyric.

The sign (appearance, clothing, possessions or instruments of the personage), the signal (which defines or forecasts the significance of actions), and the structure (such as the journey, the combat, the garden, the castle) are not used by the Duke of Orleans in any extensive sense. His writings are characterized by lack of mnemonic detail (signs), sustained actions (interpreted by signals), but occasionally he does cast cluster of poems in a setting (a court of love, a banquet) which would be a structure.

Williams' work represents the most elaborate typology of the allegorical mode, and portions of it are applicable to Charles' poetry. It will be most useful in determining the extent to which Charles' rhetoric should be called allegory, as opposed to metaphor.

All theorists (Kellogg, Steele, Owen, Fletcher, Lewis, Williams) subscribe to B. W. Montgomery's two traditions of allegorical research: "the rhetorical definition inherited from Quintillian and

---

[20] Arnold Williams, "Medieval Allegory: An Operational Approach," *Poetic Theory/Poetic Practice, Papers of the Midwest Modern Language Association* I (1969), p. 78.

the exegetical method of reading on two or more levels of meaning."[21] The critics also unite to lament the absence of clear analyses of the subtle and sophisticated proliferations of rhetoric, and they all share an insistence upon duality of meaning. From this selective review of studies treating allegory, three major conclusions emerge:

1. All allegorical writing depends, for content, on two or more levels of meaning.

2. Sufficient analysis of rhetoric is wanting.

3. Critical apparatus valid for treating the narrative may not suit the short lyric as well.

It is now appropriate to determine what insights relevant to these three points have come from a rather considerable body of scholarship dealing with the poetry of Charles d'Orléans. First, what is the inner message, expressed through the more obvious surface one — the content of his writing.

Scholars examining the love poems of the long-exiled thrice-wed Duke have been attracted by the possible correspondance between historic event and poetic content; they have sought a concrete actuality as the deep motivation and inner meaning of creation. Beaufils writes:

> Sa position ne lui permettait pas d'exhaler ouvertement ses plaintes; mais il pouvait à titre d'amoureux, peindre à sa dame imaginaire tous les sentiments qui agitaient son cœur: c'est ce qu'il fit et ce qu'il ne cessa de faire que quand sa dernière espérance se fut évanouie. (p. 116)

According to Beaufils, the Duke was driven to allegory as a device of concealment, for his personal safety during the imprisonment in England. But, as if to contradict this interpretation, the allegorical mode persisted into the later works, written in times of total freedom and marital concord when the birth of children publicly heralded and celebrated was scarcely compatible with secrecy. For the patriotic or political verse, written between the years of 1415

---

[21] Robert L. Montgomery Jr., "Allegory and the Incredible Fable: The Italian View from Dante to Tasso," *PMLA*, 81 (1966), p. 45.

and 1440, allegory may properly be interpreted as an expedient tool for hiding real truths.

There are also, in Charles d'Orléans' works, incidental writings, in allegorical form, for specific occasions. Charles d'Héricault notes that the *Poëme de la Prison* contains "*nombre de ballades qui sont réelement un récit, un envoi, une offrande*" related "*à tel fait vraiment arrivé, à telle impression ressentie à un moment précis, et à la suite d'un incident réel.*"[22] These are circumstantial, and that they can be situated precisely in physical life in no way increases or diminishes our understanding of the rhetoric of allegory in the other poems. For the most part, Héricault's conclusion is true: the allegorical poem is usually "*une œuvre de pure imagination*" (p. xxix).

Alfred Glauser's comprehension of the peculiar relationship between poet and poem is highly suggestive. Writing about Ronsard and mindful of the quantity of effort and attention focused on the authentic Cassandre, Glauser maintains

> La Cassandre d'un "sonnet pour Cassandre" n'a jamais existé. Ronsard trouvait plus de femmes dans les sonnets que dans les allées des jardins. Par eux, il a appris à faire sa cour; il leur demande un secret d'existence. En écrivant, il songeait moins à Cassandre qu'au sonnet pour Cassandre. (p. 16)

Instead of being the deeper meaning of the allegorical poem, events may cause the writing, even suggest the hierarchy of concepts and images, but, in Glauser's words "*le poème-symbole absorbe les éléments d'une vie, les oublie et se substitue à eux*" (p. 16). The poet is seen as "*victime*" and "*maître*" of his creation, at the same time "*séduit par elle, mais la dominant*" (p. 8). The poem, escaped from the chains of mere circumstances, becomes "*une réalité vivante et saine.*"

Insofar as studies of the dual meaning of allegory's content have dwelt upon the identification of actual events and mysterious ladies for the ballades, they have contributed background useful in fixing particular personal references and imagery based upon

---

[22] Charles Joseph de Ricault Héricault, *Poésies complètes de Charles d'Orléans* (Paris: Flammarion, n. d.) I, xxix.

daily matter, but it should be recognized that they have offered little in terms of an understanding of the workings of allegory. It is important to consider the poem as a technical literary creation by an artist, beyond the intriguing and colorful circumstances in which the poet lived and to which he responded. The allegorical mode is not primarily a means to privacy but a vehicle for more interesting artistry.

Four contemporary scholars have attempted to determine or describe the content of Charles' poetry: Victoria Lebovics (1962), Norma Lorre Goodrich (1967), Daniel Poirion (1965), and John Fox (1969).

Lebovics seeks to reveal "the complex of values which informed the poet's view of life, those things which he held to be important or valuable," [23] and she carefully builds an argument holding that the death of the Dukes' beloved serves as catalyst in the principal intellectual crisis of his artistic life: his rejection of courtly love. The attitude toward courtly love is then the center around which other values rotate in changing equilibria at various stage of his life and experience.

Goodrich finds nine themes (Identification, Craftsmanship, Allegory, The Peerless Lady, The Eyes and What they See, War and Peace, Death and Old Age, and Philosophy),[24] and she concludes, after tracing their development in French and English verse, that Charles' mind was "susceptible of isolation and separate scrutiny" (p. 209), that it questioned and studied in "a search deriving its impulsion... from a basic dissatisfaction with truths as presently available or patently presented" (p. 210), and that it was both introverted and introspective (p. 210).

These two perceptive works, linked with Daniel Poirion's vast analysis of the leading fifteenth century poet-princes, are comprehensive in scope, and while each has a certain thesis to prove (the rejection of courtly love, the authorship of the English poems, or a certain socio-artistic grouping with its own common traits and differences), each illumines yet another facet of Charles' inner

---

[23] Victoria Lebovics, "The Moral Universe of Charles d'Orléans," Diss. Yale 1962.
[24] Norma Lorre Goodrich, *Charles of Orleans, A Study of Themes in His French and in His English Poetry* (Geneva: Droz, 1967).

world, moral, thematic, or cultural. Each work sees Charles' poetry through the lens of the late Middle Ages, highly polished by historical distance, and each also sees the times through the Duke's writings. For the most part, allegory means a rhetorical mode or set of devices to these scholars, and Goodrich defines her "theme" of Allegory as the attempt to conceptualize be personification certain inner processes, which processes are most interesting to her.

Sir John Fox, composing a study of Charles' lyric poetry,[25] seeks to be all-embracing, treating biography and literary history, rhetoric (allegory and medieval style), textual analysis (the ballades and rondels) and the sound schemes of short works. There is no section dealing with meaning as distinct from form, for Fox rarely separates the two, but on every page the reader deepens his knowledge of Charles' ideas and their interpretation.

If content has been interestingly presented by a set of capable critics, what of the second problem, the analysis of rhetoric and the functioning of allegory?

The concept of Charles d'Orléans as allegorist has been evident at every stage of critical consideration of his work. Beaufils, one of the earliest commentators, saw in the poet a Son of the Rose, competent and even creatively representative of an era when allegory was the rule. Yet, Beaufils does not define the term nor does he differentiate allegory in the narrative from allegory in the lyric.

Ferdinand Kühl, in 1886, produced a monograph entitled *Die allegorischen Gestalten Karls von Orléans,* in effect nothing more than an annotated alphabetical list of personified abstractions. Daniel Poirion's *Le Lexique dans les Ballades de Charles d'Orléans* (1967) is a similar lexical inventory, published eighty years later under the influence of technological innovation and its felicitous attributes of accuracy and inclusiveness. In such works there is no theory or explanation of the functioning of allegory.

Pierre Champion is certainly the first scholar to open many aspects of the literary history of this poet: texts carefully edited, biography correlated with literary production, and criticism that

---

[25] John Fox, *The Lyric Poetry of Charles d'Orléans* (Cambridge: Cambridge Univ. Press, 1969).

is both erudite and sensitive. If he displays confidence in the historico-biographical method and a preference for the life-and-works approach, the results can scarcely be faulted for the vast amounts of data united with insight which they contain. Yet, Champion too perpetuates elegantly the legend of Charles the Allegorist without pausing to question its validity nor to expose its substance.

Robert Steele, by opening a Pandora's box of English verse attributed to the Duke of Orleans, revealed for the first time longer works, where plot and incident occur.[26] It is after the publication of the excellent edition by Steele that one might expect critical evaluation of allegory to begin to change; but since there is no tradition of separating allegory in the narrative (source of most theories about its function) from allegory in the short lyric, Steele's book did not prove to be the turning point it might have been. It did destroy eventually the parochial vision of Charles as monolingual or bilingual (Latin being assumed for a learned aristocrat of his status and time), but did not stimulate inquiry into the nature of the poet's *"perpétuelle allégorie."*

Three critical works subsequent to Steele contain sophisticated commentary on the function of allegory in the works of this poet — books by Cigada, Goodrich, and Fox. Though the primary interest of each study is not rhetoric, each scholar in turn weaves his particular inquiry on matters rhetorical into the greater fabric of arguments he or she considers to be essential. From a careful reading of their analyses, several suggestive threads appear for further investigation: 1) is Charles d'Orléans properly considered a poet of allegory at all (Cigada)? 2) can the charge that his allegorical figures are not fully committed (Fox) be substantiated or documented consistently? 3) is there any aesthetic reason why his personified abstractions appear less clearly formed or articulated than those of his favorite allegorical source, *Le Roman de la Rose* (Fox)? Until these threads are followed to successful

---

[26] Robert Steele, *The English Poems of Charles of Orleans,* Early English Text Society, Series 215 (Oxford: Oxford Univ. Press, 1941). Robert Steele and Mabel Day, *The English Poems of Charles of Orleans,* Early English Text Society, Series 220 (Oxford: Oxford Univ. Press, 1946). All quotations from English poetry by Charles d'Orléans are from the Steele edition and follow the numbering of items used by Steele.

conclusions, the problem of rhetoric remains partially unsolved and the role of allegory in the short lyric is an unknown quantity.

Studies of medieval allegory have led us to feel that Dante is the great medieval craftsman for this techniques or mode, the epitome not only of achievement but also of possibility. The *Divina Commedia* and the *Roman de la Rose* stand like the pillars of Hercules, and the temptation is to view other allegorical verse as a trivial reflection or partial imitation of the more mighty accomplishments. As prolonged narratives, they are generically different from the short lyric, which exhibits its own merits and subtleties. It is hoped that this study will prove enlightening with respect to the sustained metaphor in the short lyric, the poetic achievements of Charles d'Orléans, the potentialities of medieval allegory in many genres, the execution of courtly verse, and those sequences of creative acts that constitute the transition from the Middle Ages to the Renaissance.

II

THE WORKINGS OF RHETORIC

Allegory and Metaphor

Like the critical opinions or definitions of allegory, its use may vary within the works of an author; any poet's writings may be technically successful because of his mastery of the device or conversely they may fail in a particular instance on account of his ineptness at control of rhetoric. Charles d'Orléans often turns to an allegorical mode of expression, though not always with identical aesthetic intentions or ever fortunate results. There appear to be levels of usage and degrees of proficiency in his works. To examine these, two working definitions are indispensable: first, a notion of allegory applicable to the lyric; and second, a concept of metaphor, allegory's principal gloss.

In spite of the wealth of later efforts and an apparent *embarras du choix*, Coleridge's definition offers a breadth of scope rendering it highly applicable:

> We may then safely define allegorical writing as employment of one set of agents and images with actions and accompaniments correspondent, so as to convey, while in disguise, either moral qualities or conceptions of the mind that are not in themselves objects of the senses, or other images, agents, actions, fortunes, and circumstances so that the difference is everywhere presented to the eye or imagination, while the likeness suggested to the mind; and this connectedly, so that the parts combine to form a consistent whole.[1]

---

[1] S. T. Coleridge, *Miscellaneous Criticism*, ed. T. M. Raysor (Cambridge: Harvard Univ. Press, 1936), p. 30.

Such a definition will permit the inclusion of abstractions, personifications, and conventional figures from the contemporaneous literary tradition, all of which are found in the works of this poet.

The cardinal guise of allegory is the metaphor; since allegorical narratives are designated "extended metaphor," the fleeting metaphor becomes an allegory *en capsule*. The role of this device, whether it is limited to ornament or inflated to greater importance and interest, is all-important. Arnold Hauser defines metaphor as:

> ...indirect, figurative speech that, instead of a familiar and usual expression, applies another that is less usual and is as surprising as possible...[2]

The language of Charles d'Orléans is highly figurative and indirect: he is a master of metaphor, which may involve personification and which is frequently interpreted by his critics as allegory.

Hauser continues:

> ...in comparison with the symbol, the allegory, or the parable, it is direct speech, however, because though it results in a devious instead of a straightforward and obvious description, it does not in the least modify the original meaning of the thing described, and adds nothing to what would have been said by the familiar expression. (p. 391)

In these terms, the abstract, figurative, even ornamental manner of the Duke of Orleans is indeed more metaphor than allegory: the "devious" description does not modify meaning, no matter how much it may enhance, ennoble, enrich a concept whose expression in familiar language would have been aesthetically unacceptable to the fifteenth century courtly poet. Does Charles ever permit his figures allegorical freedom, that is to escape and feign a life of their own, becoming "something else"; or does he keep firmly under his control so that they become translations, better expressing his mood, tone, or feeling than plain language? Do they, like any other rhetorical device used well, facilitate and contribute to the communication stylistically though not primarily amplifying it or

---

[2] Arnold Hauser, *Mannerism* (London: Routledge and Kegan Paul, 1965), p. 391.

altering it in content? These questions are but logical extensions of the main problem — is this writing allegory or not?

Goodrich has observed,

> When we speak of allegory in the poetry of Orleans, we mean only that he attempts by personification, sometimes successfully and sometimes unsuccessfully, to conceptualize certain inner processes — a standard poetic mode of his day. (*Themes*, p. 67)

Yet, while recognizing it, Goodrich does not seek to explore the nuanced terrain of allegory, personification, and metaphor, where the three intersect or overlap, or offer varying avenues for interesting poetizing, resulting from the poet's choice of one or the other. Identification of the subtleties permitted by these three and the subsequent exploitation of their potential will contribute greatly to the success of Charles' verses; confusion and clumsiness will result in failure, or a less successful poem.

Rondeau XXXI "*Le temps a laissié son manteau*," widely anthologized, is said to exemplify full allegory typical of this period and clearly employed. The poem's central image is personification; there is an incident or event described whereby the non-human is given personal attributes, belongings, and actions. Yet, the subject it not abstract nor is its language highly figurative; it does not represent the conceptualization of inner processes. The use of *Temps* is surprising, for *Natura* in female form was a more conventional literary personification and was accessible to Charles through any number of texts in his library. Instead of allegory, this rondeau provides almost a classic example of metaphor. It illustrates well the poet's understanding of the technique of personifying, and a short lyric based on the proliferation of a single, simple image. The reputation it has is well deserved, for it is surely aesthetically successful.

The Development of Allegorical Figures

Charles d'Orléans uses allegorical figures in single undeveloped references, in passages of three of four lines, and through a framework which may support an entire poem. Occasionally an abstraction is merely named to create an atmosphere, to summarize a mood; the language is clearly figurative and metaphorical, but the existence of allegory is debatable. Examples from Ballades I and XI will illustrate.

Ballade I: Se si a plain vous vois mes maulx disant,
Force d'Amours me fait ainsi parler; (vv. 9-10)

Ballade XI: Loingtain de vous, ma tresbelle maistresse,
Fors que de cueur que laissie je vous ay,
Acompaignie de Dueil et de Tristesse, (vv. 1-3)
... trouveray, se m'a dit Esperance, (v. 8)
...
Autant de bien que j'ay de desplaisance (v. 10)

En attendant le guerdon de Liesse (v. 23)
...
... le conseil de Loyaute feray, (v. 25)

The words *Force d'Amours, Dueil, Tristesse, Esperance, Liesse, Loyaute,* each used only once, represent psychological postures or feelings; they serve to situate the poet in an intellectual world. The reference is frugal, unsustained, a cameo metaphor in miniature, colorful but terse. By refusing to elaborate on any of the abstractions, Charles preserves the centrality of the poem's content and preoccupation for another subject, in this case himself in a suppliant attitude toward his sweetheart.

Other poems contain the allegorical figure briefly developed, for a few lines or a stanza. Ballade XXI will serve as an example.

Ballade XXXI

Venes vers moy, Bonne Nouvelle,
Pour mon las cueur reconforter,
Contez moy comment fait la belle:
L'avez vous point oy parler
De moy, et amy me nommer?
A elle point mis en oubly
Ce qu'il lui pleut de m'acorder,
Quant me donna le nom d'amy? (vv. 1-8)

From the first three lines, where *Bonne Nouvelle* is the object of the imperative, followed by the question directed specifically to *Bonne Nouvelle* as *vous,* Charles shifts to a query not specifically aimed but whose echoing form (interrogative) and vocabulary *(nommer-nom, amy-amy)* sustain the earlier overt presence of the allegorical figure. Subsequent stanzas do not refer to *Bonne Nouvelle* again. The turn of rhetoric is far more effective than would be plain language; not only is it appealing in ingenuity or novelty, but the grammatical or linguistic arrangement of the strophe's ideas is rich. The last five lines are a restatement in the interrogative or reversed (negative) form of the very news he wishes to hear.

In other poems, the allegory spills out beyond a single stanza to permeate the entire ballade. For example, Ballade XXIV is based on location, and the territory or place represents a mood; since the words occur in the refrain, they are repeated and provide a setting or framework for the whole message:

Ballade XXIV

Mon cueur au derrain entrera
Ou paradis des amoureux;
Autrement tort fait lui sera,
Car il a de maulx doloreux
Plus d'un cent, non pas un ou deux,
Pour servir sa belle maistresse,
Et le tient Dangier, le crueulx,
Ou purgatoire de Tristesse.

Ainsi l'a tenu, long temps a,
Ce faulx traistre, vilain, hideux;
Espoir dit que hors le mettra
Et que n'en soye ja doubteux.
Mais trop y met, dont je me deulx;
Dieu doint qu'il tiengne sa promesse
Vers lui, tant est angoisseux
Ou purgatoire de Tristesse!

Amour grant aumosne fera,
En ce fait cy, d'estre piteux,
Et bon exemple moustrera
A toutes celles et a ceulx
Qui le servent, quant desireux
Le verront, par sa grant humblesse,
D'aidier ce povre soufreteux
Ou purgatoire de Tristesse.

Amour! faittes moy si eureux
Que mettez mon cueur en liesse;
Laissiez Dangier et Dueil tous seulx
Ou purgatoire de Tristesse.

Tristesse, Dangier, Espoir, Amour are the abstractions: *Amour* is addressed or prayed to as god of love, capable of interceding for the lover or releasing him; *Espoir* is the friendly counselor, ministering to the prisoner; *Dangier* is his demon tormentor, along with *Dueil*; all find themselves in the purgatory of *Tristesse*, that is, sadness is both compared to purgatory and is the prevailing mental state of purgatory in the construction that is one of Charles' favorite techniques.

The differences in emphasis, development, or prominence given to the allegorical figures in the writings of this poet indicate sensitivity to the potential of the device, creativity and sophistication in the task of poetizing, beyond slavish mimicry or mere versifying. The Duke of Orleans controls the personifications he creates or perpetrates, and the space or importance he gives them is one guide through the uncertain area between metaphor and allegory, a region he infinitely prefers.

The differences in emphasis, development, or prominence given to the allegorical figures in the writings of this poet indicate sensitivity to the potential of the device, creativity and sophistication in the task of poetizing, beyond slavish mimicry or mere versifying. The Duke of Orleans conrols the personifications he creates or perpetrates, and the space or importance he gives them is one guide through the uncertain area between metaphor and allegory, a region he infinitely prefers.

Not only does Charles develop the rhetoric of each poem differently, there are different uses of allegory and metaphor apparent within individual poems. It is interesting to note his way of following other authors in the use of conventions, his ability to exploit the difference between person and personification, his variety of manipulations of a collection of capitalized abstractions within a single brief lyric, his use of dialogue or speech as a means of personifying, and particular patterns of metaphor typical of his verses. Each of these clearly involves the "set of agents" or images stated to be the requisites of allegorical writing by Coleridge, while the "consistent whole" is always a goal of Charles, fully cognizant as he is of the inner unity and cohesion of the short lyric.

The Conventions of Heart and Eyes

By the fifteenth century, there are several conventional figures or phrases inherited by the poet; the Duke of Orleans as an avid reader of poetry and eager collector of manuscripts, knew these common formulae well, and his vocabulary shows a high proportion of such items.[3] Courtly love, incarnate in the lyric poetry Charles admired and perpetrated, provided a rich set of such conventions, as did the writings of religion, also of more than passing interest to him.

Like many of his peers, he often selected the heart as an alter-ego or convenient expression for his feelings; already in this chapter we have observed several examples of this kind of allegorizing, but Ballade XLIII illustrates well the personification of the heart in contrast to the poet himself.

Ballade XLIII

Mon cueur est devenu hermite
En l'ermitage de Pensee;
Car Fortune, la tresdespite,
Qui l'a hay mainte journee,
S'est nouvellement aliee,
Contre lui, avecques Tristesse,
Et l'ont banny hors de Lyesse;
Place n'a ou puist demourer,
Fors ou boys de Merencolie:
Il est content de s'i logier;
Si lui dis je que s'est folie.

Mainte parolle lui ay ditte,
Mais il ne l'a point escoutee;
Mon parler riens ne lui proufite,
Sa voulente y est fermee,
De legier ne seroit changee.
Il se gouverne par Destresse
Qui, contre son prouffit, ne cesse,
Nuit et jour, de le conseiller;
De si pres lui tient compaignie

---

[3] For an alphabetical tabulation of all vocabulary in the ballades, see Daniel Poirion, *Le Lexique de Charles d'Orléans dans les ballades,* Publications romanes et françaises, No. XCI (Geneva: Droz, 1967).

Qu'il ne peut ennuy delaissier:
Si lui dis je que c'est folie.

Pour ce sachiez, je m'en acquitte,
Belle tresloyaument amee,
Se lectre ne lui est escripte
Par vous ou nouvelle mandee,
Dont sa doleur soit allegee,
Il a fait son veu et promesse
De renoncer a la richesse
De Plaisir et de Doulx Penser,
Et apres ce, toute sa vie,
L'abit de Desconfort porter:
Si lui dis je que c'est folie.

Si par vous n'est, Belle sans per,
Pour quelque chose que lui die,
Mon cueur ne se veult conforter;
Si lui dis je que c'est folie.

In addition to the half-dozen or more capitalized abstractions, there are three full people in this ballade: the lady, the poet, and the heart. All three are distinct; and the poet's posture of judgment on the resoluteness of the heart's chosen situation is qualified by a tone of amusement that is detaching as well as detached. At no point are the *je* voice and the *cueur* one and the same; Charles has successfully captured and portrayed man's ability to evaluate his own actions through this convenient rhetoric.

The personification is accomplished through the first line's metaphor; the heart has become a *hermite,* the only personalizing noun in all three stanzas and the Envoi. Charles repeats the concept of the word by using a derivative in a metaphor of place, *l'ermitage de Pensee,* a phrase structure echoed twice in later lines — *ou boys de Merencolie* and *l'abit de Desconfort.* The heart is of the same status as other conventional personifications *(Fortune, Tristesse, Destresse, Plaisir, Doulx Penser),* with whom he interacts; the poet does not belong to their group, does not address them, and speaks of them only in relation to their peer, the heart. The heart is active throughout the verses, though the primary deeds involve attitude, or communications: *il est content, il ne l'a point escoutee, sa voulunte y est fermee, il se gouverne par Destresse, ... il ne peut ennuy delaissier, il a fait son veu et promesse, ... ne se veult conforter.* The heart does not actually perform any physical act, even those potentially appropriate to the hermit, nor is the human analogy of the hermit's life exploited. *Fortune* and *Tristesse* have affected the heart, the poet has spoken to him, the lady is interested to send him a word, all marks of his individual nature, while simultaneously creating that independence. The supportive, subsidiary imagery is based lexically on diplomacy and communication: the former (involving participles *tray, aliee,* and *banny*) describes the accomplishments of *Tristesse* and *Fortune,* and it is perhaps significant that the quiescent side of contact between enemies is depicted not the violence of open combat. The *Roman de la Rose*'s bellicose setting almost necessitates, as well as supports, movement and firmly outlined anthropomorphic figures, as opposed to the shadowy suggestions of allegorical beings found in Charles' writings. The imagery of communication concerns the desired exchange between the heart and lady, which the poet smilingly intercedes to procure.

What did the writer gain through use of this particular rhetorical device? He has rendered the structure of the ballade more complicated by adding a third party, given a third dimension, truly the third, which results in depth through complexity. The content of the poem becomes more interesting and is thereby improved.

Another device, similar to the use of the heart as alter-ego, is the relationship between the heart and eyes, used ever since Ovid to portray the inception of love. An early ballade by Charles will illustrate his use of this tradition.

Ballade IV

Comment se peut un povre cueur deffendre,
Quant deux beaulx yeulx le viennent assaillir?
Le cueur est seul, desarme, nu et tendre,
Et les yeulx sont bien armez de plaisir;
Contre tous deux ne pourroit pie tenir;
Amour aussi est de leur aliance;
Nul ne tendroit contre telle puissance.

Il lui couvient ou mourir ou se rendre
Trop grant honte lui seroit de fuir.
Plus baudement les oseroit attendre,

S'il eust pavais dont il se peust couvrir;
Mais point n'en a, si lui vault mieulx souffrir
Et se mettre tout en leur gouvernance:
Nul ne tendroit contre telle puissance.

Qu'il soit ainsi bien le me fist aprandre
Ma maistresse, mon souverain desir.
Quant il lui pleut ja pieça entreprandre
De me vouloir de ses doulx yeulx ferir;
Oncques depuis mon cueur ne peut guerir,
Car lors fut il desconfit a oultrance;
Nul ne tendroit contre telle puissance.

The poet philosophizes on the beginnings of love and his inability as Every Lover to resist its power. The two persons of the poem, the suitor and his lady, appear in the last stanza only; after they have entered upon the scene, the reader is well aware that the allegorical figures have prepared the way, rhetorically and conceptually. The movement of the poem involves the following juxtapositions: stanza I — a heart and two eyes are personified by the situation of warfare, in which *Amour* aids the heart; stanza II — the poet describes in human terms the feelings and alternatives for the heart in such a struggle where loss is inevitable; stanza III — the author identifies with the heart (*"mon cueur"*) and attributes the eyes to his lady (*"ses yeulx"*), and he then assumes the emotional state of the heart. We observe not only the double set of images intrinsic to the rhetorical device, but also a final merger of the two sets through which the relationship between the poet and lady (the poem's theme) is communicated unmistakeably and with intense force. It is as if Charles had deliberately bared the mechanics of personification, and the reader, apperceiving the merger of the two sets of images, consciously absorbs the technique of the rhetoric as well. The communication has certainly been enhanced and enriched by the use of the allegorical figures, conventional though they be. This is the courtly, formal poet, at his rational best.

Person versus Personification

One of the most creative facets of the rhetoric of this poet involves the contrast between personification and person; the previous ballade illustrates this well. Charles is able to manipulate figures of speech neatly and differentiate the two worlds of real existence and intellectual fantasy, profiting from their similarities and differences and balancing them off against each other. In another ballade, he accomplishes a juxtaposition through inversion, an unusual development.

Ballade XLV

Se Dieu plaist, brief ment la nuee
De ma tristesse passera,
Belle tresloyaument amee,
Et le beau temps se moustrera:
Mais savez vous quant ce sera?
Quand le doulx souleil gracieux
De vostre beaute entrera
Par les fenestres de mes yeulx.

Lors la chambre de ma pensee
De grant plaisance reluira
Et sera de joye paree,
Adonc mon cueur s'esveillera,
Qui en deuil dormy long temps a.
Plus ne dormira se m'aid Dieux,
Quant ceste clarte le ferra
Par les fenestres de mes yeulx.

Helas! quant vendra la journee
Qu'ainsi avenir me pourra?
Ma maistresse tresdesiree,
Pensez vous que brief avendra?
Car mon cueur tousjours languira
En ennuy, sans point avoir mieulx,
Jusqu'a tant que cecy verra,
Par les fenestres de mes yeulx.

De reconfort mon cueur aura
Autant que nul dessoubz les cieulx,
Belle, quant vous regardera
Par les fenestres de mes yeulx.

The persons of the ballade are four: God, named in a conventional formula; the lady; the poet; his heart. Unlike a poem discussed earlier (Ballade XLIII), the poet and his heart are not strictly separated, for the *cueur* currently sleeps in the *chambre de ma pensee*, literally internalized by the metaphor, and the poet expresses no distinct attitude or judgment of the heart.

The poet becomes in three stanzas the medium, rather than the actor or recipient: the heart will see through the poet's eyes, the lady will look through them, the *clarte* will dawn through them. The poet himself neither looks, nor sees, nor receives, but is transparent. His only act is to question the lady, and he is a person reduced to a hollow personification.

The lady is *tresdesiree*, described as *amee*, endowed with a *doulx souleil gracieux*, the transmitter of *clarte*, and simply *belle*. She also does not act, but is instead static, and though actions are suggested around her, at the end of the third stanza she is the future recipient of the look of the heart through the eyes of the poet; like him, the lady is devoid of movement, a personification. In sharp contrast to the lady or the poet, the heart is given a physical existence in metaphoric physical surroundings, it performs as a human, and awaits transformation when it will awaken to a room of *joye*, gleaming with *plaisance*. In a neat reversal, the abstractions are alive while the poet and lady are empty; this condition is strengthened by the metaphors characterizing emotions or qualities, *la nuee de ma tristesse, le doulx souleil gracieux de vostre beaute, le beau temps* or *la journee*.

Allegorical figures are most common to medieval didactic or moralizing literature, and to the narrative. When the abstract quality is personified, clothed, and given other human attributes, it can be remembered better. Yet, in the lyric, with no didactic or moralizing purpose, with no sustained and sustaining narrative, how does the personification function? The purpose of the lyric is the depiction of a striking image, to convey a theme or evoke a mood; to fulfill this goal in a brief space Charles skillfully controls selected abstract nouns, and some become full personifications while others remain suggestive shadows. Ballade XLIII (*supra*, pp. 43-44) may serve as an example.

As was noted earlier, the heart is fully personified from the opening line, willful, active, garbed in an *abit*, literate, deliberately uncommunicative, and contrasted to the poet and lady. There are also eleven other abstractions, treated in varying ways: *ennuy, doleur; Plaisir, Doulx Penser; Desconfort, Pensee, Merencolie; Lyesse; Tristesse; Destresse;* and *Fortune*. These constitute a hierarchy of sorts beginning with *ennuy* and *doleur,* psychological conditions which are named purely and simply, signaled linguistically by the minuscule initial letter. *Plaisir* and *Doulx Penser* are slightly removed from the first level toward complete personification in a type of phrase construction which the poet often uses to render the abstraction more human, but the noun to which they are linked is *richesse,* itself an abstraction and completely a-personal. *Desconfort,* on the other hand, is bound to a potentially personifying noun, *abit;* but since the mantle itself is *Desconfort,* any separate figurative existence is denied by the metaphor, and an abstraction becomes an attribute, not a personification. *Pensee* and *Merencolie* are associated with location; *Lyesse* is the kernel of an elided metaphor of the same type. *Tristesse* seems to have an identity because of its relationship to *Fortune,* but in fact this is only a reflection, since *Tristesse* achieves no independent status and is merely designated companion. *Fortune* is modified as *tres-despite,* acts *(s'est aliee)* and constitutes an entity with a psyche of her own *(a hay)* and durative existence *(mainte journee, nouvellement).* With the mere mention of her name, her physical shape and appearance are conjured up, particularly for a medieval audience. *Destresse* is given a similar portrait composed of like traits. Of the eleven abstractions, only two exhibit human characteristics or behavior.

The Duke of Orleans barely sketches the outlines of many of his personifications, and his frugality of presentation is essential to the short lyric. He gains needed space and time by touching first one and then another abstractions, never painting in full, and always being highly selective; he chooses elements for the ballade on the basis of their contribution to the overall unity and content, then for stylistic improvement through the rapport between images. The hierarchy of levels of personifications is a fine example of this type of composition, at which Charles is a master.

Dialogue and Speech

Most of the verses by Charles d'Orléans are descriptive statements or questions, but some contain quoted speeches. Such a citation may be attributed to a personification, as in Ballade **XXXVII** where *Espoir* is given a direct statement, or Ballade XXXVI where *Ennuy* speaks a few lines. In Ballade XLVII the refrain is a quotation, while in Ballade LVI, the poet's quoted words compose the second stanza and the heart's reply makes up the third. Speech is one of the most typical of personifying techniques; in the *Roman de la Rose,* there is a clear distinction made by the poet between images, in human guise, outside the *Jardin de Deduit,* who are not alive, do not move, and do not speak, and the true allegorical figures inside the garden, who are given the faculty of language and converse with one another. The morality plays of the late Middle Ages frequently contained abstractions who appeared on stage, performed all manner of actions and, naturally, spoke. In a sense, it is strange that Charles does not employ this device more often; yet, his chosen genre is the short lyric, not the drama any more than it is the narrative, and the forays he does make into dialogue are well-executed. The length of the ballades and their somewhat more formal or elevated tone separate them from the rondeaux, and it seems appropriate to consider dialogue in each form separately, the ballades first.

Two ballades illustrate the use Charles makes of speech: Ballade LXII, a dialogue between the poet and a flower, and Ballade XXXIII, a conversation between the lover and his heart. The former contains narrative comments, very similar to the ones incorporated in the metered text of medieval verse drama as stage directions, but the latter is an uninterrupted series of brief exchanges.

Ballade LXII

Le lendemain du premier jour de May,
Dedens mon lit ainsi que je dormoye,
Au point du jour m'avint que je songay
Que devant moy une fleur je veoye
Qui me disoit: "Ami, je me souloye
En toy fier, car pieça mon party
Tu tenoies, mais mis l'as en oubly,
En soustenant le fueille contre moy;
J'ay merveille que tu veulx faire ainsi:
Riens n'ay meffait, se pense je, vers toy."

Tout esbahy alors je me trouvay,
Si respondy, au mieulx que je savoye:
"Tresbelle fleur, oncques je ne pensay

Faire chose qui desplaire te doye:
Se, pour esbat, Aventure m'envoye
Que je serve la fueille cest an cy,
Doy je pour tant estre de toy banny?
Nennil certes, je fais comme je doy:
Et se je tiens le party qu'ay choisy,
Riens n'ay meffait, ce pense je, vers toy.

"Car non pour tant, honneur te porteray
De bon vouloir, quelque part que je soye,
Tout pour l'amour d'une fleur que j'amay
Ou temps passe. Dieu doint que je la voye
En Paradis, apres ma mort, en joye!
Et pour ce, fleur, chierement je te pry,
Ne te plains plus, car cause n'as pourquoy,
Puis que je fais ainsi que tenu suy:
Rien n'ay meffait, ce pense je, vers toy.

"La verite est telle que je dy,
J'en fais juge Amour, le puissant roy;
Tresdoulce fleur, point ne te cry mercy,
Riens n'ay meffait, se pense je, vers toy!"

The setting of LXII is reminiscent of the opening scenes of the *Roman de la Rose* or the *Booke of the Duchesse,* and the extraordinary speaking flower is clearly fantasy, part of the dream; the poet himself does not act in this sequence, but merely listens and replies. In the poem immediately preceding this one (LXI) he has taken a leaf to wear as a token of faithfulness to the lady (who has died) for the coming year. In addition to the dream framework, the author uses the court of love motif, in the Envoi, where the lover plans to take his case before Love, the powerful king, who will presumably decide in his behalf. The trial scene is not presented in subsequent poems, and the flower does not appear again. The first theme of the poem is steadfastness in grief. The flower wonders why the lover has preferred the leaf to a flower, a more conventional sign in love poetry representing both the beloved and passion. The poet defends himself through Adventure, whose charge he is obeying, and by relating that The Flower, used metaphorically, is dead in Paradise. (The frequent medieval notion of a Paradise of flower-souls immediately comes to mind.) Through the distinction between the dead flower-lady and the leaf of the poet, and the speaking flower, the second theme appears:

the poet rejects the notion of consolation from another lady, and offers, in order to justify this rejection, to procure the judgment of the God of Love.

Is there any personification in this poem? Only insofar as the flower speaks, and speech is a human quality. Charles chooses one personalizing element to accomplish the personification. That the two exchanges reflect or hide a possible real dialogue between Charles the man and an unknown lady seeking his attentions is suggested by the text, but can not be substantiated. If this is true, he has employed a means of expression highly appropriate to his message, and the use of direct quotation is the result of a fortunate and effective rhetorical choice.

Ballade XXXIII

L'AMANT.	Se je vous dy bonne nouvelle,
	Mon cueur, que voulez vous donner?
LE CUEUR.	—Elle pourroit bien estre telle
	Que moult chier la vueil acheter.
L'AMANT.	—Nul guerdon n'en quier demander.
LE CUEUR.	—Dittes tost doncques, je vous prie,
	J'ay grant desir de la savoir.
L'AMANT.	—C'est de vostre Dame et amye
	Qui loyaument fait son devoir.
LE CUEUR.	—Que me savez vous dire d'elle
	Dont me puisse reconforter?
L'AMANT.	—Je vous dy, sans que plus le celle,
	Qu'elle vient par deça la mer.
LE CUEUR.	—Dittes vous vray, sans me moquer?
L'AMANT.	—Quil, je le vous certiffie,
	Et dit que c'est pour vous veoir.
LE CUEUR.	—Amour, humblement j'en mercie,
	Qui loyaument fait son devoir.
L'AMANT.	—Que pourroit plus faire la belle
	Que de tant pour vous se pener?
LE CUEUR.	—Loyaute soustient ma querelle
	Qui lui fait faire sans doubter.
L'AMANT.	—Pensez doncques de bien l'amer.
LE CUEUR.	—Si ferez je, toute ma vie,
	Sans changier, de tout mon povair.
L'AMANT.	—Bien doit estre dame chierie,
	Qui loyaument fait son devoir.

Ballade XXXIII is a perfectly balanced distribution of speeches, in three nine-line stanzas; the odd number of lines forces an alternation of speakers for the refrain from strophe to strophe, and Charles uses the pivotal fifth line of each stanza for a one-line remark upon which the repartee hinges. The pattern is thus:

SPEAKER   SPEAKER
   A - 2 lines (query)   B - 2 lines (query)
   B - 2 lines   A - 2 lines
   A - 1 line   B - 1 line
   B - 2 lines   A - 2 lines
   A - 2 lines   B - 2 lines

                SPEAKER
                   A - 2 lines (query)
                   B - 2 lines
                   A - 1 line
                   B - 2 lines
                   A - 2 lines

There is a continuity from one stanza to the next, in that at each opening the alternate speaker's turn has come up, but there is also an overriding concept of stanzaic unity rendered syntactically by the two-line question which always opens the stanza, and the normal repeated refrain which closes it.[4] In this context, the dialogue is only another feature of formal complexity, of obvious interest to the poet.

The theme of the poem is the reward of devotion and loyalty in love, conveyed by the example of the lady and the news of her impending arrival announced to the heart by the lover. Clearly

---

[4] This display of equilibrium and awareness of structure is reminiscent of the Provençal tradition where such patterning is typical and even more intricate. The lineal rhymes are identical from stanza to stanza also:

        a - elle
        b - er
        a - elle
        b - er
        b - er
        c - ie
        d - oir
        c - ie
        d - oir

the heart is here a separate being, and the possible interior relationship to the lover is not mentioned or suggested, beyond the second line *("Mon cueur")*. To achieve separation, the poet makes several assumptions: 1) the heart is ignorant of the news which the lover knows; 2) the heart has private resources; 3) the lover might trick or deceive the heart. The human lover is superior in knowledge of information, in disposing of that knowledge at his will, and in advising the heart; he also opens and closes the poem. The heart is linked with other personifications in two instances, thanking Amour and commenting that Loyaute is sustaining his case. The lover is allied to the other human of the ballade, the lady.

The creation of roles is clearly a technique of personification; it is here put to good use, making the poem's form more interesting, emphasizing formal balance, and it is technically satisfying. Rhetorically by employing the inner voice in conversation with the ego, Charles achieves depth and a certain amount of novelty within a fixed tradition.

In the rondeaux, the tone is often more conversational or informal, and there are more examples of the spoken form: eight rondeaux contain direct quotations. Some of the uses resemble those in the ballades, such as Rondeau **CLIX** which contains only two verses in quotation marks:

> "Vous estes paie pour ce jour
> Puis qu'avez eu ung doulx regart." (vv. 1-2)

Rondeau **CCVII** is an exchange of questions and replies between the lover and his beloved, but the dialogue form is not particularly well employed and does not contribute markedly to the poem's content or effectiveness. Another rondeau (**CCIII**) is composed of banter on an almost unidentifiable trivial theme, and could be called incidental; Rondeau **CCXLIII** is similar to Ballade **XXXIII** in form, since it is a scene between *Cueur* and *Soussy*, but it is not so neatly constructed as the ballade. Rondeau **CCXLII**'s conversation between the heart and the eyes is a clever exploitation of the half line, and the tone of intimacy is achieved partially through the use of sentence fragments common to familiar talk between close friends, as stanza one illustrates:

Cuer, qu'esse la? —Ce sommes nous, voz yeux.
—Qu'aportez vous? —Grand foison de nouvelles.
—Quelles sont ilz? —Amoureuses et belles.
—Je n'e vueil point. —Voire? —Non, se
  m'aist Dieux. (vv. 1-4)

Two other rondeaux are somewhat innovative in technique: CXCVIII's first line *"Mort de moy! vous y jouez vous?" (in medias res)* is a common stage opening to arrest interest, and it represents a possibility in content made available only through use of the direct quotation; and Rondeau CCLXXVII shows *Merencolie,* depicted through the speeches as outside the door, again a situation conveyed only through the use of dialogue, and not only colorful but enhancing to the poem's theme. In this last instance, speech is the crucial personifying trait, and the setting selected by the poet is one where identity is purely aural.

Rondeau CCCLI is so significantly different from the others as to merit examination in some detail:

Rondeau CCCLI

(D)'Espoir? Il n'en est nouvelles.
—Qui le dit? —Merencolie.
—Elle ment. —Je le vous nye.
—A! a! vous tenez ses querelles!

—Non faiz, mais parolles telles
Courent, je vous certiffie.
(D)'Espoir? (Il n'en est nouvelles.
—Qui le dit? —Merencolie.)

—Parlons doncques d'aultres. —Quelles?
—De celles dont je me rie.
—Peu j'en sçay. —Or je vous prie
Que m'en contez des plus belles.
—D'Espoir? (Il n'en est nouvelles.)

In the poem there are two voices, both unidentified; they speak of two abstractions, neither one of which has any attributes other than existence in the speech of two undefined parties: *Merencolie's* only trait is her ability to lie; as for *Espoir,* presumably only that which has existence can vanish leaving no news. The poet's judgment *"Peu j'en sçay"* is an accurate reflection of the reader's state at the end of the poem; he cannot define either the voices or the abstractions with any precision. All of the vocabulary and principal images are dealing with communications: *nouvelles, dit, ment, nye, parolles, certiffie, parlons, je me rie, contez.* Charles is careful to choose phrases dealing with the medium, which becomes the message in this rondeau. The tone is light, the content is certainly less serious than that of the more formal ballades, but the dialogue form constitutes the major element of levity, and ease of manner leads to the assumption of a less heavy theme.

After examining both ballades and rondeaux, one can conclude that though he does not use direct speech often, the Duke of Orleans appears to be capable of exploiting quotation or dialogue as another means of personifying abstractions and making his communication stylistically successful.

Phrasal Metaphors

In the Duke's verse, metaphors (potentially allegory) are frequently couched in a phrase structure, NOUN + de + ABSTRACTION; the pattern is so common as to be typical of this poet, and it becomes a creative and effective rhetorical tool. The process is generally a type of concretizing or fixing of the abstraction; it may involve personification or characterization in human terms, but more often it deals with a physical object, a location. In most instances, the abstraction makes its sole appearance for an entire poem in this phrase, and though there may be as many as five such constructions in a given ballade, usually there is only one. The content is not fixed, neither is there any further repetition of either element of the association in the whole body of verses. Two rare recurrences illustrate the flexible role of each member of the phrase:

Ballade CII	au hault Paradis de Plaisance	(v. 12)
Ballade LXXX	l'arbre de Plaisance	(v. 3)
Ballade XXIII	l'uis d'Amours	(v. 18)
Ballade LXV	la fievre d'Amours	(v. 3)
	du vent d'Amours	(v. 16)

Within the mold of the structure, Charles places whatever striking elements suit the theme and execution of his poem as a unity.

In such phrases *de* may show possession of the first item by the second, or identity where the abstraction is the best description, characterization or realization of the first noun.

>*Ballade CXIX*   En la chambre de ma pensee   (v. 1)
>(possession)
>*Ballade LXVI*   Sur le dur lit d'Ennuieuse Pensee (v. 8)
>(description)
>*Ballade LXIX*   mains sierges de Soupirs Piteux   (v. 5)
>(description)

Possession is definitely difficult to establish in these constructions; far more often the phrase is a pure metaphor.

In some poems, the first noun of the phrase is a part of the body or product of bodily function: hands, eyes, tears.

>*Ballade CXXII*   es mains de Merencolie   (v. 8)
>*Ballade CXXI*   Es mains de ma Dame Viellesse   (v. 3)
>*Ballade XXXV*   Des yeulx de Joyeuse Plaisance   (v. 16)
>*Ballade XXXII*   Je l'ay souventesfois lave
>En larmes de Piteux Penser; (vv. 10-11)

The above examples are not selections, but rather the sole occurrences in the 123 French ballades. Since in none of the examples is the abstraction repeated in later lines, nor is the personification continued or expanded further, it is clear that Charles is far from interested in the expansion of metaphor into "real" allegory. Personification is a rhetorical trope for him, greatly restricted in its usage though frequent in its appearance. Rather, the facts that 1) such phrases are a prevalent linguistic trait of his verse, 2) they always center on an abstraction, 3) the abstraction is only rarely personified, and 4) it is more often concretized in objects or places, lead to an assessment of his verses as containing a plethora of metaphors based on concretization of abstractions, only one aspect of which is personification.

Bestiaries, Lapidaries, Armor, Castles and Ships

Along with personification, there are other means of conveying double or inner meaning used during this period. Often in medieval writing, a stone or animal is used to represent an abstract quality;

the many lapidaries and bestiaries testify to the popularity of such symbols and the currency of their meanings. The Duke of Orleans only once uses this tool so frequently employed by most of his predecessors and peers:

> *Ballade LXIX*   ... saffir est nomme la jame
> De Loyaute   (vv. 14-15)

On another occasion he selects the convention of symbolic armor, a standard practice at least since the writings of the Apostle Paul:

> *Ballade CVIII*   Portant harnoys rouillé de Nonchaloir,
> Sus monture foulee de Foiblesse,
> Mal abille de Desireus Vouloir
> On m'a croizé, aux montres de Liesse,
> Comme cassé des gaiges de Jeunesse. (vv. 1-5)

This example is the only occurrence of allegorized armor in all of his writings. Clothing and color of apparel given customary symbolic meaning are common in the short lyrics and the longer ensembles.

Charles d'Orléans describes a castle in terms of its component abstractions concretized architecturally:

> *Ballade L* ...
> J'enforcis mon chastel tousjours
> Appelle Joyeuse Plaisance,
> Assis sur roche d'Esperance;
> Avitaillie l'ay de Confort: (vv. 2-5)
> ...
> En ce chastel y a trois tours,
> Dont l'une se nomme Fiance
> D'avoir briefment loyal secours,
> Et la seconde Souvenance,
> La tierce Ferme Desirance.   (vv. 9-13)
> ...

And the popular symbolic ship with miscellaneous nautical trappings appears on at least one occasion (Ballade XCVIII): "*De Confort la voille, ... l'eau de Fortune, ... ou bateau du Monde, ... avirons d'Espoir ... les vagues de Tourment ...*" Like the castle, this ship occurs but once in the whole poetic corpus, a singular rarity for a medieval writer devoted to allegory.

It would be a sin of omission to neglect his most memorable metaphors, which are topographic: (Ballade CV) "... *la forest de Longue Actente,* ... *Ou voyage de Desiriers,* ... *la cite de Destinee,* ... *L'ostellerie de Pensee* ..."

Does this kind of use of metaphor constitute allegory? In that there are clearly two sets of images, one an abstraction and one physical reality, perhaps; yet the associations between the two groups are fleeting, gossamer and tenuous, and because of their subordinate role in the organic unity of the poem, they seem a very fragile, brief allegory, more comfortable under the less grandiose rubric of metaphor.

Conclusions

The poetry of Charles d'Orléans is replete with abstractions, many of which are personifications, all of which are metaphors of one type or another, and some of which cannot easily be classified as allegorical figures though they may participate in a dual atmosphere (real-intellectual, external-internal). These abstractions can be discussed linguistically, their grammatical function or appearance constituting one clue to their allegorical nature. The Duke of Orleans, like any other poet, exhibits varying degrees of rhetorical success, and/or experience, poetically; his use of rhetoric is one gauge of his maturity and ability.

Within the corpus of his collected works, on various occasions, he devotes more or less attention to abstractions and expands their function to a greater or lesser degree. It is possible to observe many aspects of his creativity in adapting, elaborating, or subduing the conventional figures of his poetic inheritance; the subtlety of his intellect is revealed by his ability to contrast personification against person, and his sensitivity to the potentialities of human speech in the creation of allegory. Finally, the phrasal metaphors become an effective tool within the short lyric which demands restraint, parsimony of expression accompanied by rich colors and texture. These are the hallmarks of Charles d'Orléans.

III

MORT IN A BILINGUAL BALLADE SERIES

An analysis of rhetoric needs a smaller terrain than the complete works if it is to make any claim to depth as well as generality. For Charles d'Orléans and allegory, a most fortunate sequence of poems exists which include the figure *Mort*. Though the poetic usage varies from one lyric to another, these ballades constitute a thematic unity, a chronological segment, and a suitable entity for examination of technique. The poems (numbered LV-LXX in French and 55-72 in English [1]) express a common theme: the poet's grief, despair, and depression caused by the death of his lady. Although the identity of the lady is debated, the artistic time of composition is generally accepted as midway in the total writings of this author: they were completed during his imprisonment in England, where he wrote 94 of his approximately 155 ballades. Charles was twenty-one at the time of his capture, and was released twenty-five years later (1415-1441). The series was composed around his thirtieth year, 1425.

The unity of the sequence is primarily thematic, and the numbering of the lyrics in French, edited by Champion, does not correspond with that in English, edited by Steele. Discrepancies are the result of four poems written only in one language (58, 59, 60, 62). Table I matches the ballade numbering in the two languages.

---

[1] Roman numerals indicate French ballades, after Champion, and Arabic numbers are used for English ballades, after Steele.

French	English
LV	55
LVI	56
LVII	57
	58
	59
	60
LVIII	61
	62
LIX	63
LX	64
LXI	65
LXII	66
LXIII	70
LXIV	69
LXV	71
LXVI	72
LXVII	107
LXVIII	101
LXIX	67
LXX	68

TABLE I

Two French poems, LXVII and LXVIII, are dubious members of the series in content and execution, and the fact that their English counterparts are 107 and 101 respectively supports their exclusion from this study.

The words *La Mort, Mort* or *Deth* do not occur in six ballades of the sequence: LVI-56, an expression of the false hope that the lady is regaining her health; LVIII-61, a chess game with *Dangier* and *Fortune* lost by the poet; 62, a treatment of the phoenix motif; LXIV-69, an expression of the generalization that "all is lost," the result of the lady's death which itself is not mentioned; LXV-71, in which the poet seeks healing from the wound love has dealt him; LXIX-67, the funeral of the lady, an atmosphere of death where Death personified does not actually appear. Yet each of these poems belongs to the grouping on the subject of the lady's death. Table II lists the texts of particular concern in this examination of the rhetorical figure *Mort*.

Mort occurs in passages of varying length and occupies a position of differing importance in each poem in the series, as a brief review of citations will demonstrate.

Poem	Stanza Verse	
LV-55	I-8	... il (cueur) souaide piteusement *la mort* Et dit qu'il est ennuye de sa vie
	E-3	Que vous (Dieu) souffrez que *la mort* son effort Face sur lui (cueur), car il en est d'accord Et dit qu'il est ennuye de sa vie!
LVII-57	I-1	Las! *Mort* qui t'a fait si hardie De prendre la noble Princesse...
	II-3	Je prye a Dieu qu'il te maudie *Faulse Mort,*
LIX-63	I-6	Car *Mort* l'a mise soubz la lame Et l'a hors de ce monde ostee:
LX-64	II-5	Mais, au derrain, en son domaine *La Mort* les (dames) prist piteusement;
	III-1	*La Mort* a voulu et vouldroit, ..., mettre sa paine De destruire, ..., Liesse et Plaisance Mondaine, Quant tant de belles dames maine Hors du monde;
	E-2	*Mort* vous (Amour) guerrie fellement
LXI-65	II-3	Car, puis que par *Mort* perdu ay La fleur,
LXII-66	III-4	... Dieu doint que je la voye En Paradis, apres ma *mort,* en joye!
LXIII-70	III-3	C'est par la *Mort* qui fait a tous rudesse Qui m'a tollu celle que tant amoye
LXVI-72	III-6	... *Mort,* qui m'a trahy, A prins mon per
LXX-68	I-1	Puis que *Mort* a prins ma maistresse
58	I-3	Now *deth* allas hath to my discomfort Enrayfid memy lady and maystres
	III-3	O cursid *deth* whi nelt thou du me sterue
59	III-1	Alone *deth* com take me here anoon
	5	Alone most welcome *deth* do thi rudenes
60	I-7	... sith *deth* hath my lady
	II-5	Syn *deth* allas hath tane my lady bright

TABLE II

This listing of quotations shows that in the set, there is only one reference to *Mort* which is clearly not a personification, LXII-66, where the poet speaks of his death to come in some undetermined future. The phrase *apres ma mort* is used to contrast most vividly with the preceding word, *Paradis,* and the following, *en joye.* The tragedy of the lady's death opposes the anticipated death of the poet associated with the pure joy of the second meeting. The English version's "In paradice the howre of my deiyng" is less neatly structured, but still poetically satisfying. Yet, neither French nor English are concerned with *Mort* personified.

Rhetorical Role

Most occurrences of *Mort* are matter-of-fact references or formulae (LV-55, LVI-56, LXX-68, 58, 59, 60), and though death is clearly an active force, either described as perpetrating a deed or called upon to act, the lexicon is conventional (verbs "to take" or "to do"), consistent, and there are no personal attributes given to the abstraction. Throughout Ballade LXI-65 the poet uses a traditional floral imagery, and the formula is consequently slightly modified, so that Death appears the indirect agent, while the primary interest of the line is the poet who has lost the Flower. In these uses, Charles shows his acceptance of a system of expression, and a whole group of abstractions of his age; he is not particularly innovative, and the formula is used in a supportive manner, deliberately unobtrusive, receiving no special attention from poet or reader.

Ballade LXIII-70 shows *Mort* in a slightly different stage: the philosophical generalization, perhaps formulaic at this time. Certainly the rudeness of death is conventional, as is its universal impartiality, but the composition of these lines may be the assembling of customary ideas and phrases devised by the Duke of Orleans himself. He clearly wishes to devote more attention to death, expressing its actions in a general sense and in his own private circumstances, and the generality is a step away in conceit and form from the purely formulaic.

In Ballade LIX-63, *la Mort* occurs in a brief metaphor of particular strength; the *lame* or lid of the tomb is a real object, and though this is not a possession of Death personified, it suggests the human circumstances and rituals of death with such precision as to accomplish a personification both vividly and economically. Both parts of the image are spatial, *"soubz la lame,"* *"hors de ce monde,"* the former graphic and limited, the latter vague, vast, and otherworldly.

Throughout the first two stanzas of Ballade LVII-57, *Mort* is addressed, a striking contrast with the majority of poems in this series where death is merely named. The poet uses the familiar *tu* form, bravely accosts death from the opening line, yet, after the second stanza, *Mort* does not recur in the poem. This usage is different from the formulaic or conventional, but again Death is part of the setting for the ballade, or its linguistic framework, rather than playing a major role in the lyric's development. Ballade LVII-57 is like LXX-68 in this regard: death is named in the opening line, never to be mentioned or exploited again.

Though both instances of the word deth are formulaic in Ballade 60, the poem is particularly rich in wordplay and conscious use of grammatical categories in the formal structuring of lines. The verses display the poet well, and show his mastery of rhetoric well.

Ballade 60

For dedy lijf my lyvy deth y wite
For ese of payne in payne of ese y dye
For lengthe of woo/woo lengtith me so lite
That quyk y dye/and yet as ded lyue y
Thus nygh certeyne that y vncerteyne seche
Which is the deth sith deth hath my lady
O wofulle wrecche o wrecche lesse onys thi speche

O gost formatt yelde vp thi breth attones
O karkas faynt take from this lijf thi flight
O bollid hert forbrest thou with thi grones
O mestid eyen whi fayle ye not yowre sight
Syn deth allas hath tane my lady bright
And left this world without on to her leche
To lete me lyue ye do me gret vnright
O wofulle wrecche o wrecche lesse onys thi speche

What is this lijf a lijf or deth y lede
Nay certes deth in lijf is liklynes
For though y fayne me port of lustihede

Yet inward lo it sleth me my distres
For fro me fledde is ioy and alle gladnes
That y may say in alle this world so reche
As y/is noon of payne and hevynes
O wofulle wrecche o wrecche lesse onys thi speche

Ther nys no thing sauf deth to do me day
That may of me the woofulle paynes eche
But wolde y dey/allas yet y ne may
O wofulle wrecche o wrecche lesse onys thi speche

    The major device used is antithesis or union of opposites which is operative in each line of the first stanza. Even the refrain contrasts the poet as lyricist "wofulle wrecche" with the self-conscious, grief-stricken lover who finds the poem inadequate "o wrecche lesse onys thi speeche," desiring silence. The only departure from the tone and principal style of the opening eight lines is the phrase "sith deth hath my lady" which does not balance the preceding "Which is the deth" as neatly as do the other remarkably equal language pairs of earlier lines ("dedy lijf - lyvy deth," "ese of payne - payne of ese," "lengthe of woo - woo lengtith," "quyk y dye - as ded lyve y," "nygh a-fer - fer is ny," "thing certeyne - yncerteyne"). The phrase seems uneven precisely because of the heaviness or grand aura latent in the formula involving Death; because of the frequent pictorial and linguistic portrayals of a figure or being "Death," the word carries residual imagery, potentially present or hovering when not deliberately exploited by the poet. This is what makes the difference between "the deth" of the first half of line seven and "deth" of the second half, personal versus the almost-personified powerful abstraction.

    The second stanza develops the physical potential of I-7's use of deth, with a sequence of four lines in which a person or symbol of a whole person, rather than a quality or emotion, is evoked: "gost," "karkas," hert," "eyen." The antithesis is continued as the ghost is called to give up "breth," which the ghost typically does not have, the naturally heavy carcass is urged to take flight, while the bold heart groans and the misted eyes do not fail in sight. After these perfectly symmetrical lines, the figure Death, now stronger and more forceful, recurs, in language that echoes and expands the earlier reference:

> I-7   sith deth hath my lady
> II-5 Syn deth allas hath tane my lady bright

Each grammatical element in the first phrase has been lengthened or intensified by the addition of a modifier of some sort. This line is not bipartite, has no antithesis, and therefore necessitates the following line, itself a rather quiet and total comparison:

> II-6 And left this world without on to her leche

The next sentence is addressed to someone, though the hearer is not identified: the line describes the highest boon of a court of law "To lete my lyue" as "great vnright"; since death is not anywhere characterized as a judge, the poet is wise to leave "ye" vague, merely implying by context that it may be death.

The third stanza, while still displaying the poet's choice of the line as the primary unit of his doubling or antithesis, contains greater variety in technique. The opening two lines are in three segments; the two outer play similar roles in the content of the line and in their relationship to the middle phrases which themselves contain the opposites in immediate juxtaposition.

> What is this lijf / a lijf - or - deth / y lede
> Nay certes / deth - in - lijf / is liklynes

Similarly, in the next two lines, "fayne" is comparable to "inward" in meaning within the images and in lineal position, while "y me port" is a perfect match for "it sleth me." Lines five through seven are a unit, no single line of which supports an antithetical expression; yet III-5 "ioy and alle gladnes" is equal to "payne and hevynes," the ironic riches of this world, of which the poet has more than any other person.

The Envoi is used for echoing words of the ballade's main stanzas: deth, woofulle, paynes, allas. It states the author's inability to achieve his goal, his desire for death, his discomfort, but it is neither linguistically excellent nor so powerful in content or mood as the rest of the lyric. Though the Duke's ability to contrast the modals "wolde" and "may" is perhaps noteworthy, the second line is syntactically inadequate. Yet the ballade, in this particular series under examination, illustrates the effective elaboration of the personification Death in formulaic usage, through conscious dependence and development of its residual and conventional role.

Throughout the series, the personalia usually attributed to an abstraction for mnemonic purposes are significantly absent; the concrete nouns referring to realia relate to other human beings ("karkas," "gost," "bere," "sepulture," "testament," "last wille," "wyndyng sheet," "grave"), they are not possessions or symbols of the figure made graphic. In eight poems, death is the natural state or condition, a person's death is named, and this may be figurative (the poet's) or literal (the lady's). All forms of the verb "to die" and the adjective "dead" are also used in both ways. Charles d'Orléans, poet of *perpétuelle allégorie* at no time describes, paints, or creates a fully developed allegorical figure *Mort;* and never in this series does the personification become dominant, nor is it completely and neatly delineated, after the manner of the *Roman de la Rose* and its highly refined levels of portraiture. Linguistically and rhetorically, the poet is wholly directed to the central theme: his sorrow over the death of the lady.

Prominence and Content Role

The catalogue of citations earlier in this chapter gives little indication of the importance of *Mort* in each ballade, nor its role in conveying the major theme of the verses. The poet's attention is not always merely passing, though no single poem is devoted exclusively to Death. Not only is the importance and length of space given to *Mort* different from one piece to the next, but also the particular aspect of Death which is emphasized, that is, its role in each ballade's content. Table III provides a summary of these poems and their subjects.

POEM	SUMMARY OF CONTENT ROLE
LV-55	fear of the lady's death.
LVI-56	hope of her recovery.
LVII-57	accusation and cursing of death; formal farewell to lady.
LVIII-61	chess game with *Dangier* and *Fortune*.
LIX-63	New Year's Day gift of masses for her soul.
LX-64	vanity of the world: *ubi sunt* theme.

Poem	Summary of Content Role
LXI-65	May Day's foliage reminds the poet of the loss of his Flower.
LXII-66	the day following May Day, the poet talks with the Flower in a dream.
LXIII-70	the poet stumbles, blinded, in the forest of *Ennuyeuse Tristesse*, and talks about his mendicant status with *Amoureuse Deesse*.
LXIV-69	the poet laments his falling from the "*compagnie des amoureux*."
LXV-71	the poet, wounded by *Plaisant Beaute*, is cured by the good doctor *Nonchaloir*.
LXVI-72	St. Valentine's Day, the poet awakens in his closed chamber, lying upon the hard bed of *Ennuieuse Pensee* to hear a profusion of bird songs, and then regrets that he cannot sing with them because of the lady's death.
LXVII-107	irrelevant.
LXVIII-101	irrelevant.
LXIX-67	the lady's funeral.
LXX-68	the poet gives his testament "*Devant tous loyaulx amoureux*" and vows to remain in the chapel of *Loyauté*.
58	all diversion sleeps since the lady's death, and the poet longs for death.
59	"Alone am y and wille to be alone."
60	antithesis to express the poet's situation and feelings.
61-LVIII	chess game with Daungere and Fortune.
62	the poet extols the lady's rarity, like the phoenix.

TABLE III

The greatest lineal space is found in Ballade LVII-57, where Death is addressed through two stanzas. Though the abstraction is prominent and reinforced in this lyric, the author's focus is not on Death, and the refrain *("En paine, soussi et doleur")* is descriptive of his own state of mind or the lady's condition. The lover addresses God in the Envoi, and stanza III opens with the exclamation "*Las! je suy seul, sans compaignie!*" Even *Mort* is departed, as a listening presence; the sixth line, "*Mort vous serviray de cueur*," shows the concept of death the poet now wishes to stress — a condition or state, typical of and absorbed by the lady. Death is now associated completely with her and does not stand alone.

In Ballade LXI-65, a lyric whose entire imagery is centered on the Flower (the lady) and the passage of time represented by the life of a leaf, Death is treated as a phenomenon of nature, unexplained, presented without elaboration, nor accusation: as Fortune is the giver of the flower, so by Death it has been lost. This is not the typical medieval Christian concept of death, and it involves no ritual; it presents neither theological nor philosophical generalizations.

In Ballade LIX-63, with a refrain of the lover's prayer "*Je pry a Dieu qu'il en ait l'ame*," Death has put the lady in the tomb, "*Et l'a hors de ce monde ostee.*" The other-world is more properly stressed in this context of salvation and the poet's concern for his lady after death. This is the only usage where Death, however metaphorically, and however traditional the phrasing may be, is given a concrete association — *la lame:* it suggests the frequently representational marble tomb covers of the period, with their cold, quiescent, elongated statues in repose.

On two other occasions, Death is treated philosophically or proverbially: "*La Mort qui fait a tous rudesse*" (LXIII-70) and "*Tous mourrons ou tart ou briefment*" (LXIX-67). The imagery of Ballade LXIX-67 relates to the *obsèques* of the lady, the sociocultural ritual aspects of death. The poet reviews the service, the candles, the tomb which is a veritable treasury of precious stones, the goal of Paradise of which the lady will be the primary jewel, leading to the final comment on the inevitability of death for us all, and the futility of earthly treasure. In this poem the form *Mort* does not occur; there is no personification, though the idea of death pervades this individual execution of a poem as a variation on a theme. This is typical of the whole series where the author's concern is always with his general theme and the personification of *Mort* is subordinated to the imagery of the total lyric in which it may occur, rather than receiving the full gaze of the poet's and reader's eye.

A review of the content of Ballade LX-64 makes this even more apparent.

Ballade LX

Quant Souvenir me ramentoit
La grant beauté dont estoit plaine,
Celle que mon cueur appelloit
Sa seule Dame souveraine,
De tous biens la vraye fontaine,
Qui est morte nouvellement,
Je dy, en pleurant tendrement:
Ce monde n'est que chose vaine!

Ou vieil temps grant renom couroit
De Cresseide, Yseud, Elaine
Et maintes autres qu'on nommoit
Parfaittes en beauté haultaine.
Mais, au derrain, en son demaine
La Mort les prist piteusement;
Par quoi puis veoir clerement
Ce monde n'est que chose vaine.

La Mort a voulu et vouldroit,
Bien le congnois, mettre sa paine
De destruire, s'elle povoit,
Liesse et Plaisance Mondaine,
Quant tant de belles dames maine
Hors du monde; car vrayement
San elles, a mon jugement,
Ce monde n'est que chose vaine.

Amours, pour verité certaine,
Mort vous guerrie fellement;
Se n'y trouvez amendement,
Ce monde n'est que chose vaine.

The refrain announces the major thesis: *"Ce monde n'est que chose vaine!"* The Duke of Orleans supports this premise not with realia or concrete references from the physical world, but instead the imagery of each stanza is based on an aspect of the intellectual universe.

The ballade begins with the reminders by *Souvenir* of the *"grant beauté,"* the one called by his heart *"Sa seule Dame souveraine,"* metaphorically, *"De tous biens la vraye fontaine,"* recently dead, and whose memory provokes weeping, as the poet concludes that this world is vanity. The correspondence between the fountain and the weeping poet, the sovereign lady (fountain) of all goods, memory who introduces the setting of this poem as an intellectual one, all are carefully presented concepts, in neat relationship to one another.

Stanza two begins with a mention of the *"vieil temps,"* and the fame of Creseide, Yseud, Elaine (all literary heroines), their perfect beauty, and the removal of these ladies by Death who took them to his domain, on account of which the poet concludes that by contrast, this world's land is only *"chose vaine."* [2] The emphasis is still intellectual; the removal by Death is a reminiscence of a literary figure Death, personified so frequently that it, like the heroines, is a recognizable character.

In stanza three, Death is active, willing destruction, if possible, of *Liesse* and *Plaisance Mondaine,* allegorical figures from the greater literary tradition (and states of mind), threatened by Death's insistent removal of beautiful ladies, whose absence makes the world of allegory *"chose vaine."*

The Envoi is addressed to the central figure of all allegorical writings, *Amours,* who is told that *Mort* makes treacherous war upon him, and unless he take heed to find remedy for this predicament, the world is only a vain thing. More is at stake than simply the death of a beauty or Beauty in general: Death, the intruder and destroyer from the real world, makes war upon the prime person of the intellectual world, the god of Love, chief of all allegorical creatures.

The word *mort/morte* occurs in each stanza, and the first is particularly interesting where the lady is described as *"morte nouvellement."* It is this participial usage which illustrates the purpose of the word in the poem: not to announce a personification, or an allegorical figure with interest or life of its own, but to illustrate the poet's theme or subject. The imagery refers to the intellectual sphere, and two separate types of literary performance: heroines and allegorical figures. The lady (stanza one), the heroines

---

[2] Villon's "Ballade des dames du temps jadis" within the *Grand Testament* (1465) treats the same theme and also contains names of famous women, but here the similarity ends. There is no separation of historical figure from mythological, no grouping of women according to profession or date, no attempt to interrelate the stanzas of the ballade except through the presence of the repeated refrain.

(stanza two), the allegorical figures (stanza three) are linked together by their relation to Death, by their associations with Love, whose relationship to Death (in treacherous warfare) is revealed in the Envoi. *Mort* is a lexical tool, used for a greater whole, at the command of the author; it contributes to the imagery but does not receive importance from it.

These ballades in series present differences with respect to length or prominence of reference to *Mort* and relative importance of the figure in each poem's content. Charles d'Orléans does not always devote the same amount of space to the personification or idea of death, nor does he keep the same point of view toward death from poem to poem. Metaphoric participant (LIX-63), executor of traditional actions within a customary landscape (LXI-65), literary personification adopted from allegory (LX-64), element of a philosophical generalization (LXII-66), or assumed background for the rites of the funeral (LXIX-67), *Mort* receives a variety or emphases, and each presentation is individually organized and construed.

In this series there are two poems similar to LXIX-67 (the description of the lady's *obsèques)* in that *Mort* is only an oblique subject, not specifically named: LVIII-61 and 62. Not even in a supportive role does the rhetorical device appear; each ballade reveals the self-conscious and deliberate poet whose verses are so typically crafted.

Ballade LVIII-61 presents a new context for the expression of Charles' reactions to death: the chess game with *Dangier,* aided by *Fortune.* The poet plays *"devant Amours"* and the adversary *Dangier* is described as *"faulx"* or *"cursid false,"* adjectives applied to Death in other poems of the series. The lady has been *prise,* the lover is *mat,* unless he find a new lady, *"Se je ne fais une Dame nouvelle."* His lady, as he recounts in stanza two, was his strength and succor; he laments in stanza three that Fortune will now beset him, and he himself may lose the whole great game, without a lady.

There are two strong personifications, Love and Fortune, neither one with any personalia or attributes; the naming of Love provides the climate and setting while the choice of Fortune as manipulator of the adversary makes the loss of the lady a temporary misfortune, so that it does not constitute permanent defeat of the poet. Death is suggested through vocabulary, and the lover's sadness and despair are limited to an event, this game, in time; the refrain is futuristic, and the final word *"nouvelle"* indicates an attitude of acceptance or assimilation of death as an item of the past. This attitude renders a personification not only unlikely but potentially importunate.

The refrain of Ballade LVIII-61 ("Without so by y make a lady newe") gives the opening line for Ballade 62 ("Shulde y me make a lady new Fy Fy"), but the imagery of the two poems as well as the direction of content is completely different.

The main subject is the poet's fidelity to his departed lady, and the refrain is based on the phoenix motif. The people of the ballade are the poet, the lady, the Fenyx, clerks and a knight mentioned in comparisons, no abstractions. The abject lover rejects the thought of taking another ("Nay rather dey than doon so fowl a dede" I-2), stresses the rarity of the lady, her unique nature, and reiterates the fact of her death ("She ded is" II-7, "she deyde" III-7, "she deyde, she deyde" E-4). The traditional symbol of resurrection, the phoenix, is here unassociated with the lady's afterlife, and only the bird's unusualness and unnaturalness is stressed. What reference is applied to new life deals with a general rebirth of love, for the poet, as a new sweetheart, a different person from the deceased. The poem is then dominated by a sense of the earth-bound, terminal nature of human life, as opposed to the rare mythological, even fanciful phoenix; there is no consoling faith, transcendant vision, but only an extoling of the virtues of the lady, her excellent and superlative qualities during her earthly life, accompanied by the poet's pledges of loyalty to her and his love for her. Does the phoenix refrain ("Right as the fenyx lyveth withouten ayre") suggest that he regards this constancy as also unnatural, impossible for atmospheric man who cannot live without air? Why is Death absent? The lack of personified abstractions may mean that the poet is deliberately choosing the participants, to put the phoenix in relief as the only unworldly being, and to limit the imagery to terrestrial creatures with a physical existence. In this earthly poem, death is past, and the poet is expressing his evaluation of his situation and former troth rather than discussing the death itself.

General Evaluations of Mort Applied to This Series

Death was a common personification in the literature of the Middle Ages. Italo Siciliano ranks it as comparable in power to and juxtaposed against the figure of the Virgin:

> Mais à côté d'elle (la Vierge), contre elle, le moyen-âge vit se dresser une ombre redoutable, une sombre divinité dont la puissance et la cruauté étaient aussi grandes que la puissance et la douceur de la Mère de Dieu.[3]

Pointing out the singular absence of the concept of death as liberation, (pp. 234-5) Siciliano catalogues a variety of voices, garbs, and poses given to Death, or manners of expressing various aspects of Death in literature:

> a) La Mort en personne va raconter aux spectateurs d'une moralité religieuse ce qu'elle fait souffrir à l'agonisant ...
> b) ... le spectacle du cadavre, de la charogne ...
> c) On fit parler le tombeau:
> d) On fit parler le mort dans son tombeau.
> e) ... le cadavre — ou plutôt la charogne — sans sexe et sans nom, ... "chastoie" le philosophe passant dans un cimetière:
> f) On fit sortir le cadavre du tombeau pour le porter parmi les vivants, contre les vivants.
> g) On fit parler la Mort. Hélinant, Robert le Clerc l'avaient chargée de faire une tournée édifiante de visites. D'autres lui donnèrent une figure, — squelette ou momie, — une voix, des gestes, la vie. (pp. 236-239)

In this series of ballades, the Duke of Orleans, though expressing by image and metaphor the presence and powerful effects of death, uses none of these voices, poses, or garbs; he does not recount physical suffering, but mental grief. The greatest of man's enemies, *"devant qui les hommes et même la Vierge ne peuvent rien, l'ennemi qui assombrit tout et enlève toute valeur à la richesse, à la beauté, à la puissance, à la vie elle-même,"* (Siciliano, p. 228) be-

---

[3] Italo Siciliano, *François Villon et les thèmes poétiques du moyen âge* (Paris: Colin, 1934), p. 228.

comes a figure of speech, a personification without attributes, one of many such abstractions in an intellectual universe whose ultimate triumph is the relegation of Death to the level of one concept among many. This series of poems exposing the poet's reactions to his lady's death is important for the insight it provides into the craftsmanship of Charles d'Orléans and his concept of the structure of the ballade, and the exploitation of rhetoric. *La Mort* is not developed allegorically; it is consciously placed and used within the greater framework of the complete lyric. It is subdued technically, and it receives appropriate emphasis as a part of a greater poetic whole.

Daniel Poirion comments:

> C'est au cœur du poème, au niveau même de sa structure que s'élabore vraiment l'intention formelle et expressive. La notion de *structure*, souvent invoquée par la critique moderne, désigne ici une réalité essentielle: c'est en effet la structure formelle qui nous donne le seul critère positif des genres lyriques. L'œuvre apparaît d'abord, non pas comme un "message" prétentieux ou comme une "vaticination," mais comme une certaine organisation des paroles et des pensées traditionelles, rythmée selon les lois du mouvement lyrique. (*Le Poète*, p. 9)

The use of the abstracted personification *Mort* within this series of related poems reveals a highly sensitive poetic technique; the poet appears competent, disciplined, endowed with a sense of balance and order.

IV

ALLEGORY IN THE LONGER VERSE

Because of the critical insistence on the dominance of allegory in the writings of Charles d'Orléans and the traditionally acknowledged benevolence of narrative as the most propitious setting for the flourishing of allegory, it is important to consider this poet's longer poetic productions. Although he never wrote a single developed and prolonged fiction in allegory to compare in length or scope with Spenser's *Faerie Queene* and Dante's *Divina Commedia*, he did create lengthy compositions at several stages in his artistic life. The poems where full blown allegory might be most likely to occur fall into two groups, the following individual items:

- A. *Canticum Amoris*
- B. *Le Livre contre tout peché*
- C. *La Retenue d'Amours:* French version
- D. *La Retenue d'Amours:* English version
- E. *La Songe en complainte/* Vision in Complainte
- F. Love's Renewal
- G. Five complaintes
- H. One Letter
- I. The 10-stanza "To all Lovers"
- J. The 14-stanza "End of Banquet"

and three ensembles:

- I. The Early Ballade Cycle
- II. The Banquet of Song and Dance
- III. The New Fortune

A. *Canticum Amoris*

The poem was written under Franciscan influence, and Gilbert Ouy cites several examples of Charles' debt to both English and French clerics of that order (Pierre de Blois, Wynchelsey, Gerson, Cordelier, Pierre d'Ailly).[1] It is not narrative in that there is no action or intrigue; rather the Duke here has ventured into the realm of polemic or propaganda without providing any allegorical framework to arrest the reader's interest, aid his memory, or divert him.

There are figures present; God and the members of the Trinity to whom the verse is addressed, the soul whom the poet seeks to convert, the "*créatures périssables*" contrasted with the typical persons of Christian lore (learned fathers, angels, the Virgin Mary, glorious soldiers of the church militant), and finally, the author himself. Neither portraiture nor metaphor intrude, and this is actually a rhymed treatise or profession of faith rather than a lyric narrative. Charles differentiates soul from ego and names familiar persons without depicting them, and thus the poem shows techniques typical of his shorter works; his use of allegory, characterized by restraint, suggestion, and absence of mnemonic human detail, is not determined by the length of fixed form poems he preferred but rather is a consistent feature of style.

---

[1] Gilbert Ouy, *Un Poème mystique de Charles d'Orléans, le Canticum Amoris* (Milano: Società Editrice Internazionale, 1959). Ouy has summarized the content of the poem as follows:

> Le thème central du *Canticum Amoris* est simple: le poète exhorte son âme à aimer le Créateur plus que les créatures périssables; afin de la convaincre que Dieu mérite pleinement cet amour, il énumère tous les témoignages de la solicitude du Tout-Puissant envers l'Homme: les splendeurs de l'Univers (vv. 61-108), mais aussi ces dons inappréciables que sont les facultés de l'âme (vv. 109-168) et, sur le plan surnaturel, la Grâce (vv. 185-244), la Rédemption (vv. 245-280) et surtout les béatitudes célestes, qui sont très longuement décrites (vv. 305-540). Au terme de cette visite idéale du Paradis, l'auteur invite son âme à s'élever au-dessus des vaines jouissances de ce monde pour contempler la Trinité, car c'est en elle seule que l'on peut trouver le véritable bonheur et le véritable amour (vv. 541-624) (p. 65).

B. *Le Livre contre tout peché*

Written when the poet-prince was ten years of age, these 148 lines are usually viewed as the school-boy exercises which promise in form and content the achievement, if not the style or thematic preoccupations, of the adult artist. The prologue announces his intention of writing verses to please God and instruct the reader, through reviewing the sins of pride, avarice, luxury, envy, gluttony, anger, sloth, one by one. They are not allegorized figures, but the content of each quality's passage is based on a real or religious authority incarnate: Lucifer, Cato, St. Bernard, Alain de Lille, Godefroy de Vinsauf. The stanzas are dominated by the poet himself, express his views or version of what he has been taught or thought. Animals are mentioned in the poem, with facts of natural history and geography; none of these will concern the mature Duke of Orleans, even as a leit-motif. His later use of natural objects will always be within the courtly convention, flowers, leaves, seas and winds, not interesting to man's curiosity for their own sake but rather meaningful symbols. Even as a child, Charles shows an awareness of form and orderly structure which is typical; the sections of the poem are balanced, similarly organized, and no one sin receives significantly more or less attention. The longer unity is accomplished through use of a binding prologue and epilogue, with very little to supply cohesion from within the individual sin passages, which are labeled and separated. Most significant to this study of allegory is the absence of personification, portraiture, or narrative, in spite of a dominant presence of individual abstractions. The poet's devotion to metaphor will make his later verses more figurative, and as a very young boy, he shows some intellectual biases which he will never lose, a lack of interest in some types of writing (sustained allegorical narrative) and fondness for others (short lyric).

C. *La Retenue d'Amours:* French version

This opening section of Champion's edition of the *Poésies* is a clear allegory, within a dawn vision, peopled by the God of Love and his courtiers in a setting reminiscent of the *Roman de la Rose,* where personifications speak, move, and act in other human ways.

From the opening line, with its mother-figure *Nature*, who creates Charles and then entrusts him to the protection "*D'une Dame qu'on appeloit Enfance*," to the final disposition of *Amours* who confides the smitten and ailing poet to the care of "*Espoir, mon medecin*," Charles is the only human, all of the other participants being abstractions, with the exception of two other victims of *Plaisant Beauté* named by *Amours, Sampson* and *Sal e mon*. There are two groups of personifications: first *Dame Nature* and her ladies *Dame Enfance* and *Dame Jennesse* and her messenger *Dame Aage;* then the court of the God of Love, which includes *Cupido, Venus, Plaisance, Beauté, Compaignie, Bel Acueil, Destresse, Bonne Foy, Loyauté, Espoir*. In the "*Copie de la Lettre de Retenue*" which follows the 400-line narrative, *Cupido* and *Venus* are mentioned, as are *Mondaine Liesse, Dangier, Malle Bouche, Jalousie,* and "*la cité de Gracieux Dieu.*" Of these only *Cupido* and *Venus* are also named in the longer first section.

The sparse plot is almost banal in its bareness and lack of intrigue;[2] the poet is more interested in the dialogues of his

---

[2] The story of *La Retenue d'Amours* is simple in content and structure. After two strophes to recount the Duke's birth, childhood, and arrival of youth, the adventure begins on the morning of St. Valentine's Day. *Jennesse* comes to the waking lad and informs him that they are to go meet "*un seigneur dont te fault acointer*" and who will give them "*bonne chiere.*" Charles asks the name, learns it is *le Dieu d'Amours*, fearfully states that he is too young for such torment, to which *Jennesse* replies that he knows nothing of the delights of Love and will be able to take them or leave them without constraint. The poet gets a guarantee of this freedom, they go to the "*manior Trop bel assis et plaisant a veoir,*" where the necessary formalities are exchanged with the doorman *Compaignie*. The young prince is introduced to the others and then in the place where the god's favorites are dancing, singing and amusing themselves, he meets *Amours*, to whom he expresses the medieval law of hospitality:

> Estrangier suy venu en vostre hostel,
> Honte seroit a vostre grant noblesse
> Se fait m'estoit ceans mal ou rudesse!   (ll. 188-190)

Amours promises that there will be no constraint, but also decrees that Charles will fall in love, calls *Plaisant Beauté* who shoots an arrow into the heart of the poet. The arrow has no name, and Charles attempts a defense with a thought which arrives too late. Ill, he throws himself at the feet of *Amours* who laughingly mocks his plight and easy downfall; the young Duke swears fealty to *Amours* and to the Lady Beauty who administers an oath of him in four parts, followed by six commands.

characters than their behavior. The fifteenth century reader learned little or nothing about Love's psychology from reading these lines, and certainly the traditional conventions were more elegantly and elaborately revealed in scores of other works. The echoes of the *Roman de la Rose* are not strikingly tasteful in their selection; and even such components of romance as character motivation receive uneven treatment from this poet who is convincing in his depiction of the youth's hesitation, but gives a conversion by device in the scene of Charles' falling in love which is almost as unmotivated as that of the pagan king in the *Jeu de St. Nicolas* and as frustratingly external to the human psychology as the use of the potion in the *Tristan*. The poem is, by itself, unremarkable as an example of a youthful attempt which falls short of its models.

D. *La Retenue d'Amours: English version*

Steele considers that this unit of two poems, the first of which has a French counterpart, represents a new opening for the first ballade cycle, composed during the English exile of the Duke of Orleans. The two poems are respectively a legalistic letter to Cupid and Venus, corresponding word for word to the French *Copie de la Lettre,* and an account of an interview with the God of Love concerning the release of the lover's heart, which results in the poet's decision to write ballades. The second descriptive poem is called "an entirely new introduction" to replace the first 393 lines of French narrative, a decision reached because Charles perhaps felt "the difficulty of representing himself as a shy, inexperienced youth." It cannot stand comfortably alone, because of obvious references to incidents and characters of the French (for example, the delivery of the lover's heart), and Steele's suggestion that this is a later composition might reasonably account for apparent repetitions and inconsistencies in emphasis.

Bonne Foy, secretary to *Amours,* gives him *the Lettre de retenue,* and *Amours* closes the poem with a gentle admonishment:

> Gardes tousjours ce que t'ay commande,
> Et je t'auray pour bien recommande.   (ll. 399-400)

The accompanying *Copie de la Lettre* is in four-line stanzas, legal language, has neither action nor anecdote, though several personifications are named. It ends the narrative sequence.

The second poem, in narrative, contains a plot which is neither neatly related, nor clearly formed into stanzas;[3] the author does not deal with motivation, nor does he present action well. The personifications are not described, either in stasis or movement, and the ending is merely a cessation, not a carefully prepared denouement. In these lines appear the many levels of allegorical figure which he will elsewhere deploy (the poet, the God of Love, the lady, the heart, formulaic oaths to God, personified abstractions), and there is a tantalizing stanza peopled by real flesh-and-blood commoners:

> The marchaunt wiff/nay doughter of burgeys
> With giftes grete to fresshe them in a-ray
> So maist thou when ther fauoure best y gesse
> But what a cherlis doughtir dawbid in clay
> As strokis grete not tippe. nor tapp/do way
> But loke who that most fowlist kan bigynne
> The rewdisshe child so best lo challe he wynne

Both the tone and content are reminiscent of Chaucer, one of Charles' favorites (it may be well to remember that he lodged with Chaucer's granddaughter and her husband for a time),[4] although in other instances when following Chaucer, the Duke will digest the material more completely and put it into forms and phrases more typically courtly and his own.

In comparison with the French *La Retenue d'Amours*, the English is badly written, poorly composed, and difficult to follow in plot line. It is clearly inferior, and though the French is an imitation of the *Roman de la Rose* in miniature, the English lacks the vestigial grace of form and theme from a model. If it is

---

[3] The second poem relates how the poet approached the God of Love, to ask for the return of his heart (the heart had been taken from him in the French version); the God of Love appreciates his predicament, but refuses his request. The poet then decides to petition Beauty to guard his heart carefully for a short time, while he will, with the support of Hope, compose poems to please the persons who might help him assuage his pain.

[4] Alice Chaucer, only daughter of Geoffrey's son Thomas Chaucer, was the wife of William de la Pole, third Earl of Suffolk, who was responsible for the keeping of Charles "the King's prisoner" from 1432 on. For an account of their friendship see Enid McLeod, *Charles of Orléans, Prince and Poet* (Viking: 1969), p. 186 ff.

complete and finished, this poem is a poor testimony to Charles' abilities.

E. *Vision in Complaint* / *"Songe en complainte"*

This ensemble appears in nearly identical form and sequence in English and French: a narrative section is followed by a petition, a group of ballades, and a closing letter. The intrigue centers around the poet's decision, after the death of his lady, to request his release from the service of the God of Love and retire to await Old Age's inevitable arrival before Death. Of all Charles' verse, this mixed set is the most complicated in plot and the most successful as narrative. The story is balanced in presentation, developed enough to permit a greater range of rhetorical repertoire, and complete. [5]

---

[5] The Songe opens at dusk, as the poet prepares for sleep; immediately an old man appears, whose name the Duke has forgotten, producing some shyness in the poet. The old man is *Aage,* and he relates Charles' own maturing process through the company of *Enfance, Dame Nature, Jennesse.* *Aage* describes the ridiculous figure of the old man in love, suggests that only a youth can leave the service of Love with dignity and self-respect. *Aage* then proposes that since the youth's lady love has died, he should formally ask leave of the God of Love and his court of lovers, beseech the return of his heart, then, taking care to avoid the deceptive persuasions of Fortune, retire to await *Vieillesse.* The poet awakens to the sad realization that *Aage* has warned him of the imminent approach of *Vieillesse,* whose favor he now decides to win by renouncing Love. He reflects on loving, on his youthful belief that all good lay only with love, and his juvenile ignorance of love's pains. Now he resolves to follow *Aage's* counsel, to write a formal complaint to Love, to take leave publicly, and to regain his heart. Here ends the opening section.

Part two is the *Requeste,* also composed in stanzas though of a shape which differs from that of the opening section and in a legalistic tone. This in turn gives way to the ballade series, which is in some ways more dramatic in construction than lyrical — a dialogue and tableaux intermingled. Ballade I relates the formal presentation of the *Requeste* to *Amours* who asks the lover to reconsider, to listen to Raison, and to take a new lady. In Ballade II, the lover refuses this suggestions, and Ballade III is Love's response, agreeing to release the lover from service; Ballade IV is a description of the release ceremony, the document of which is the French *Quittance* (a poem which has no English translation or counterpart). Ballades V, VI, VII contain the events immediately following the receipt of the *Quittance* document: V, the lover weeps, Love offers any favor as consolation, and assigns *Confort* to guide the lover who is speechless and blinded by his tears; VI, *Confort* is told to take the lover to the dwelling of *Nonchaloir,* which he does; VII, Tyme a-past greets the lover, hears of

Within the action of the *Songe* narrative, many allegorical figures appear, in diverse stages of personification; the first, *Aage*, is one of the few abstractions in human form ever so described in all of Charles' writings. In the English text the poet gives a one-line picture "Bifore me stonde a man with lokkis gray" in which the abstraction is clearly a person, standing, and characterized by a single salient human trait. Ironically, the Duke of Orleans continues:

> Which y not knew and yet y had him say
> For which that with my thought is writhid y
> That y so had forgote him folily
> And even for shame oon word ne durste him say

The one principal omission or deficiency in his use of allegorical figures is mnemonic detail, and in this occurrence where a personified abstraction is given precise physical shape, he states clearly that he can't remember the abstraction.[6]

The French version of this passage shows less detail, for Charles writes of *"Ung vieil homme"* (no hair color) and immediately reveals *"que point ne congnoissoye;"*. Yet this phrasing too is slightly different from his usual choice of words; he will often prefer a designation of function, such as *"messagier,"* and he rarely writes *"homme," "femme," "enfans."*[7] As the narrative

---

the parting from Love, and after a night's sleep *Confort* is sent away. The series closes with the letter written by the lover, carried by *Confort* to the God of Love and describing Charles as melancholically awaiting the arrival of *Vieillesse*, in a state of withdrawal and quiescent resignation.

In addition to the Letter, the English group also has a ninth ballade recounting the healing of the lover, in the house of No-care, by "passid tyme." This poem does have a French counterpart, but Champion situates it at yet another ballade's distance from the *Songe en complainte*, as merely another individual unit in the greater ballade collection and not part of any grouping.

[6] One instance is surely too slender a thread from which to suspend an interpretation or theory of a poet's rhetoric, but it is tantalizing to wonder whether this indicates a rejection of the whole mnemonic function of personification.

[7] Daniel Poirion, *Le Lexique de Charles d'Orléans dans les Ballades* (Geneva: Droz, 1967). Poirion lists two instances of *homme* in the whole corpus of the ballades:

LXXVI	23	Gentilz hommes avec chevalerie (the famous "Priez pour paix" ballade)
LXIII	8	L'omme esgare qui ne scet ou il va (refrain)

progresses, *Aage* is silent, then identifies himself and delivers a ten-strophe monologue, peopled first with *Enfance, Dame Nature, Jeunesse, Raison, Vieillesse, Folie, Amours,* and *Mort* who occur in phrases that Charles has used in other poems.

La Retenue d'Amours

En cest estat, par un temps me nourry;
Et apres ce, quant je fu enforcy,
Ung messagier, qui Aage s'appella,
Une lettre de creance bailla
A Enfance, de par Dame Nature,
Et si lui dist que plus la nourriture
De moy n'auroit et que Dame Jennesse
Me nourriroit et seroit ma maistresse.
Ainsi du tour Enfance delaissay
Et avecques Jennesse m'en alay.

La Songe en complainte

Un peu se teut, et puis m'araisonna,
Disant: "Amy n'avez vous de moy cure?
Je suis Aage qui lettres apporta
A Enfance, de par Dame Nature,
Quant lui chargeay que plus la nourriture
N'auroit de vous; alors vous delivra
A Jeunesse, qui gouverne vous a
Moult longuement, sans raison et mesure.

Ballade LVII (also LX, LXIII)

Las! Mort qui t'a fait si hardie,
De prendre la noble Princesse

La Songe en complainte

Puisque la Mort a prins vostre maistresse

Femme similarly appears twice:
IX   28   Elle semble, mieulx que femme, deesse;
LXXVIII   18   (Venus aussi, la tresnoble Deesse,)
                Qui sur femmes doit avoir la maistrie

Enfant is used the most sparingly of the three:
CXVI   4   (... mais c'est honte)
               Et don d'enfant, bien le savez.

ALLEGORY IN THE LONGER VERSE 85

No one of these figures is described; they are named and a reference is made to their conventional or traditional role. As personifications they depend on active verbs without picturesque detail, or on a formulaic appositive:

La Songe en complainte
Or est ainsi que Raison, qui sus tous
Doit gouverner, a fait tresgrant complainte
A Nature de Jennesse et de vous,
Disant qu'avez tous deux fait faulte mainte.
...
... Vieillesse, la mere de courrous,

In contrast to this usage are three other groups:

1) the humans of the passage about the old man enamoured; 2) *Amours* and his court; 3) the household of *Nonchaloir*. Each of these represents a slightly different or novel type of being, either real people, or an established and traditional set of imaginary imitation persons, or Charles' invention of a metaphoric household. The first group is presented in the monologue by *Aage:*

French
Et tout ainsi qu'asses est avenant
A jeunes gens en l'amoureuse voye
De temps passer, c'est aussi mal seant
Quant en amours un vieil homme folloye;
Chascun s'en rit, disant: Dieu quelle joye!
Ce foul vieillart veult devenir enfant!
Jeunes et vieulx du doy le vont moustrant,
Moquerie par tous lieux le convoye.

English
Forwhi alle suche as is hem wel sittyng
That flowre in yowthe and in ther fresshe corage
What game also make they and what skoffyng
When they se elde is falle into dotage
Saiyng o god what ioy yond drye ymage
May do vnto a fayre lady likyng
Both yong and olde thus good pei lo mokkyng
When they se elde right as a colt to rage

The French and English strophes correspond in meaning and imagery, but each has some individual peculiarities in development and juxtaposition of images. In the French lines, the Duke gives a vivid street scene, where small crowds of people laugh, point, exclaim to themselves, and the old man is met by mocking townsfolk wherever he goes. The sketch is deliberately suggestive not of the courtly ambiance, but rather the earthly, everyday fifteenth-century citizen most colorfully painted in such behavior by a Breughel, a century later. Charles d'Orléans does not often use such subjects, and in this instance, he situates them strikingly as well. The real world is allowed to intrude as if twice removed — first, by the dream sequence, and second, by its presence in the narrative of an allegorical figure *Aage*.

The English version adds to these features a subtlety in selection of images. The phrase "yond drye ymage" is chosen to characterize the old man's ridiculousness, which is thus non-human, non-allegorical, and flat like the images on the wall of the garden in the *Roman de la Rose;* then, in the last line, the comparison "right as a colt to rage" provides a third dimension (animal) in contrast to the image-like and the human. The use of an animal comparison is even rarer in the poetry of Charles d'Orléans than is the use of real people; from the world of nature he commonly prefers birds or floral imagery.[8] However, he is very fond of any typological equilibrium, and this kind of tripartite opposition is typical of his taste. Much of his success in balladeering comes from his sensitivity to the balancing of rhetorical and thematic components against one another; even in English, his natural proclivity toward this sort of structure appears.

The court of *Amours* constitutes a second grouping depicted in the *Songe en complainte*. Charles states several times that this is a *Parlement*, where all the lovers are present, that is, those who have sworn allegiance to Love. The poet declares his intent to hand over his declaration before such an assembly (lines 161-2, opening narrative), then writes the text of his formal request (*Requeste / Petition*), and finally, changing drastically the form of the poem, begins the series of ballades which will recount the scene more dramatically.

---

[8] Goodrich discusses the use of nature images, with particular emphasis on the later poems, Chapter V. The Eyes and What They See.

He spends little time or space on the setting, preferring quoted discourse for the first three ballades, then a tableau, and finally three closing ballades of intermingled narration, speech, and description of inner feelings which cannot be articulated. This sequence is the central action of the Vision in Complaint, and the middle ballade, the tableau of leave-taking is the most important in the development of the narrative's action. Here *Amours* summons his *Parlement* to whom he relates Charles' decision to take leave of their company (first strophe); Charles asks for the return of his heart (second strophe); and, kneeling, he thanks the God of Love who returns the heart wrapped in black silk (third strophe).

In the entire scene, there are only two speakers, the poet and *Amours;* one other abstraction, *Confort,* appears, to do Love's bidding. And all action takes place before the *Parlement.* No person or figure is depicted, either in physiognomy or in dress. In a sense, the poet has no more human shape than the God of Love and his agent *Confort.* Those at the court are called "*amans*" / "young folke"; they are not abstractions, nor gods, nor have they names or specific demeanors. Mention is made of Reason and of Death by both Charles and *Amours,* but the language is conventional, formulaic, and neither *Raison* nor *Mort* is a designated member of the court, though both human and abstraction recognize them as beings. Charles has taken no human friend with him to the court, and the household of Love is apparently easy to find. There is no password or ceremony to obtain admittance, and the leavetaking ritual is simple, stressing only the subservience of the lover, and presenting *Amours* as gracious, compassionate, and generous. Though Charles both speaks and weeps, the only human activity of *Amours* is speech.

How much of a court scene is really provided by the poet? He names it a *Parlement,* but does not elaborate thereon, to reinforce this designation with picturesque detail or local color; the technique is perfectly analogous to Charles' method of treating allegorical figures who are so often given names and a few human patterns of behavior conveyed by verbs, but no possessions or physical traits. In this case, the court itself is an abstraction, just like *Mort, Espoir, Tristesse,* in the ballades.

The third and final group described by the Duke is the household of *Nonchaloir,* his own metaphoric creation, the "castelle of

No care." This "aunciente cold manar // Wherein long y had in childhod lay" is found at a day's ride from the court of *Amours*, and the gate is tended by a porter who reportedly greets them after recognizing both the poet and his escort. The castle is managed by a "rewler, tyme a passid" who also welcomes Charles politely, "with glad countenaunce," and is made privy to the preceding episode. This household has much in common with the many chateaux in the romance, where a *vavasour* and his daughter or a single servant will welcome the knight adventurer, with little information given about the organization, architectural plan, or daily routine of the dwelling. The reader is left to imagine the typical *manoir*, and only the traits most important to the metaphor are evoked: the name of the castle itself and the name of its *gouverneur*. Their symbolic value is thus delimited precisely, not left to be inferred.

In this sequence, the Duke of Orleans has attempted to relate a change in outlook, self-awareness and resignation, a turning from the intense love or grief of youth; to recount this, he uses an allegorical plot line expressed in several poetic forms which contribute to the advancement of the narrative or effectively illustrate some happening. The pacing, movement, and balance of the action, its ebb and flow through succeeding waves of announced intention, narrated deed, and described event, all unite to make this work one of the poet's most satisfying productions. Unlike the loose collections of ballades on the theme of death, here the commentary accompanying the self-contained yet inter-related units and within the two or three legalistic pieces draws these separate items into a cohesive whole whose warp is an intrigue and whose woof is the varying parts in colorful juxtaposition of style and rhetoric. Allegory and personification are important elements in this success, and are particularly well controlled throughout.

F. *Love's Renewal*

Like *La Retenue d'Amours* and the *Songe en complainte*, Love's Renewal belongs to a longer ensemble; yet it is also a self-contained narrative and is deserving of individual analysis, apart from the book framework Charles has constructed for and of it in conjunction with shorter verse.

Existing only in English, the poem consists of three segments, the first a six-stanza (42 line) account of his acceptance of a commission to write a ballade for someone else, the second the ballade commissioned (in 56 lines), and the third (616 lines) a lengthy description of a dream vision followed by an outdoor fete at which Charles meets a new love, hence the title.[9] There are three women

---

[9] The story is picturesque and somewhat complicated. The Duke of Orleans states that he has been writing for others, out of boredom, and thus has accepted an assignment to compose a few lines on the subject of Fortune. He goes to the seaside, finds a great rock overlooking the ocean, and a bench on grass like a carpet. Here he composes the seven-stanza ballade which is the second part of nove's Renewal.

In the ballade, Charles laments Fortune's stability, which he observes through his constant misery. Writing in the first person, he complains that he cannot win the lady for lack of largesse and wishes for his turn at the top of Fortune's wheel.

The third part, a return to narrative, takes up immediately after the completion of the ballade-writing. Charles is fatigued from his work and he falls asleep, only to begin to dream. He will record this dream, like Macrobius' description of King Scipio; this dream is, he feels, a prediction of what will happen later, not mere fantasy, as other condescendingly classify dreams. At once the first lady appears and the poet reiterates his sleep-state, lest we forget. The lady is called naked, though wrapped about the waist with a piece of fine lawn, accompanied by many doves, and hoyding on her wrist an owl; Charles goes to the edge of the sea to meet her, and it seems to him that he is awake! It is Venus, as some of her symbolic accoutrements had suggested, and the Duke chats with her throughout twenty-four stanzas, discussing her comfort in the water, his own apparel, his sorrow at the death of his lady, and Venus replies to his protestations of inability to love again.

Just as it would seem that Venus is convincing him, the poet espies a chair of gold, drawn by two white steeds, and driven by a Queen, wearing a crown and holding a wheel. There is some confusion in Charles' mind and words as to whether she *is* his ladylove who had died, and her beauty strikes Charles mute. Venus shakes him, as he stands silent, and finally the poet suggests that Venus pretend to stoop down to pick up something and thus glance at the lady surreptitiously. Venus does so and blushes in awareness of the compromising situation, her own nakedness, their lack of a chaperon; she tells Charles of woman's greater sensitivity to such potentially dangerous occurrences. She further informs him that this is Lady Fortune, and compliments his taste, comparing him to a merchant with a fine eye for value in merchandise. Charles tells Venus, in answer to a direct query, that he loves his late lady first, this Queen Fortune next, and he begs Venus' forgiveness for this probable offense. Venus is then about to help him reach up to touch Queen Fortune when he awakens, a piece of fine material in his hand. The appearance of Queen Fortune is described through thirty stanzas.

portrayed — Venus, the goddess Fortune, and the new lady love — as well as the party on the green. The personages converse in speeches spilling from one stanza to another; the women are carefully described physically, and their words with the Duke vray in tone from banter or coquetry to sympathetic advice.

G. *Five Complaintes*
H. *One Letter*

These pieces exhibit striking stylistic similarities: the five French *Complaintes* and the English letter are all in stanzaic form (six to fifteen strophes each), and of medium length (less than one-hundred and fifty lines); each is addressed to a specific party, either real (Fredet, the lady) or symbolic (France, *Amours*) from the Duke personally. Only one has a refrain, and one is in spoken dialogue form. Personifications occur as images, participants or points of reference and are used with this poet's customary ease and frequency. Two of the six (*Complainte* III and the Letter) are used in The New Fortune.[10]

Reflecting about his unusual afternoon, the Duke starts home only to encounter a group of young people playing a game on the green; amazingly enough, one of the women looks exactly like Queen Fortune. Through a friend, who inadvertently involves him in the game, Charles meets the lady, declares his love for her, and they decide that he will write to her. The end of the game signals the termination of their conversation, but they exchange promises as the company takes formal leave. Charles records that the following night his heart was distressed all night long, and ends this surprising story with his decision to write poems for his new lady.

[10] *Complainte I:* The poet begs France to return to peace through repentance; by making Humility her lawyer, she can assure a favorable response from God and the Virgin Mary. Charles invokes feudal and religious, papal and legendary power in concrete terms to support his plea to *"Trescretien, franc royaume de France!"* and the theme of peace is consistently double-edged, both political and religious.

Complainte II: Charles pleads with *Amours* on behalf of his heart who is in the prison of *Discomfort* under the warden *Dangier* who is unnecessarily cruel. The heart feeds on the pears of *angoisse*, drinks tears, sleeps on the bed of *Pensee*, as he wears the black of *Tristesse*, the irons of *Destresse*. *Espoir, Plaisance,* are not there, and the heart desires *Mercy*. The Duke is asking release and the banishment of *Dangier* and his retainers on a safe-conduct for the heart to see his lady.

Complainte III: Charles laments his distant separation from the lady; though he was mute at their parting, he will serve her forever.

Complainte IV: The Duke of Orleans answers a letter from his friend Fredet, advising him that the service of Love is always painful, and

This assortment is useful in a consideration of the longer and narrative writings because of its possible transitional and intermediate character. Within these six there is the expanded ballade, the demi-dramatic (almost a debate or playlet) and the demi-narrative. The major trait of all six is that none truly escapes Charles' instinctive preference for the short lyric, and none of them truly stands on its own. Yet, each shows what a short lyric could have become with more space for development. An example is *Complainte* II whose allegorical expressions are more numerous and more explicit than the short ballade or rondeau permit. Yet the framework of poet as intercessor to *Amours* on behalf of his heart, in confinement, occurs in the short verses, and here the personification is not depicted in any more detail. Neither thematically nor in composition does Charles exploit the potential which expansion might afford. The *Complaintes* and Letter are more fluent, more leisurely, but not stylistically different from the ballades, rondeaux, caroles, and other short poems.

I. *Ten-Stanza "To All Lovers"*

The tight organisation of these ten strophes almost compensates for their inferiority in language; the author's sense of phrasing, and consequently his imagery, are weak at times, and though the overall movement may be well-conceived, the line-by-line progress is difficult to absorb. The Duke is writing to wish a lover well in his affairs, while also offering a few guidelines and specific pointers for the successful outcome any true lover seeks. The poem has no allegorical figures, although the God of Love is twice

---

Orleans will loyally do for Fredet whatever may help. In his turn, Charles is under the gouvernance of *Soussy* who watches his every move, and Charles hopes Fredet will give profitable advice in return.

Complainte V: In the presence of *Souvenir*, Charles and the *Prince des amoureux* engage in a formal debate concerning Love's harsh treatment of the suitor. The lover is without *Espoir, Plaisant Desir* and *Bel Acueil*, and his heart left the service of the god of Love because *Secours* was denied him. *Amours* dismisses the charges preemptorily after a flirtation with the semblance of reasonable judgment, concluding the exchange of opinions with no formal ending to the poem.

Letter: The Duke of Orleans apologizes for his rude, hasty reply to the lady's equally impulsive writing. He affirms his eternal fidelity and ends on a note of hope.

mentioned as a source of help to the faltering, and Charles also names Argus of the hundred eyes.

J. *Fourteen-Stanza "End of Banquet"*

Composed as an after-dinner reading, this poem is based on a pun from the word wesshe (meaning "to wish" or "to wash"). The poet will make wishes to entertain the company; he undertakes this commission even though he is in great torment because death has taken his lady.

In a novel form of praising the lady, the poet desires to become the incarnation of male virtue, to correspond in every degree or trait to her female perfection. Graceful, loving of honor, fair, purposive, discreet, courteous — all the ideal qualities are first mentioned, though not here personified either fully or in suggestion; the focus is on the two people being compared and their moral, emotional, behavioral description. After six such stanzas there are two about the Duke's four foes who will perhaps become his friends: daunger, drede, payne, and deth. The poet projects appropriate transformations for three of the four: daunger into grace, drede into sewrte, payne into gladnes. For deth no such possibility is imagined; heaviness substitutes for deth to make up the quartet, and a change from heavines o joy is wished. This suppression of deth (whose embodiment in convention is sufficiently strong to support a formulaic reference) provides a key to the allegorical value of the four foes: the other three are mere named abstractions, not personifications nor traditional figures. The poet avoids any instrusion by a rhetorical personage in this banquet setting with its actual human audience, the poet, and his lady.

The Ensembles:

    I. The Early Ballade Cycle.
    II. The Banquet of Song and Dance.
    III. The New Fortune.

The ensembles present different aesthetic problems and types of results than does the segmented narrative. Three disparate yet similar examples by other authors, the *Divina Commedia,* the *Vita Nuova,* and Christine de Pisan's *Cent Ballades,* all have different structural opportunities and potential satisfactions, though each one (like these three works by the Duke of Orleans) is composed of isolable constituents. What is the role of the allegorical mode in contributing to ensemble unity?

Steele is able to discern in the first sequence of ballades a coherent story, both in the French and English versions: "the history of a love affair between Charles and an unnamed lady, her death, and his abjuration of love ... set in an allegorical frame of service rendered to the god of Love and accepted by him, and of a formal renouncement of allegiance in a parliament of love" (Series 215, p. xxx). The progress of the love story is the source of movement and tension, and the death of the lady, slightly past midway in the sequence, is the pivotal event marking the high point from which the denouement will evolve. Allegorical figures are the major constituents of the supportive frame, within which Charles situates the exposure of his inner feelings, the principal subject of the set. Neither figures nor the lady are ever described; she is idealized, the assumed polestar for the Duke's behavior, while they provide a familiar background, which is itself a great source of cohesion. The allegorical mode is used here to furnish a form of landscape.

The Banquet of Song and Dance is an entertainment consisting of an introduction, invitation, ninety-six rondeaux, and two closing narrative pieces, followed by what Steele takes to be "a number of short essays in new metrical forms, perhaps dance forms, and three caroles" (Series 215, pp. xxxi-xxxii). Steele labels it "incoherent" as a result of the "several changes in its composition"; it definitely shows an unfinished air, though not devoid of grace and elegant charm which later critics so often wish to see in courtly verse. The allegorical references are sporadic and contribute nothing special to the overall effect of the grouping.

The New Fortune, third ensemble, consists of a three-part narrative, many ballades, and a letter in the midst of the shorter verse. The poet describes how he met his new lady, through the dream vision including a full portrait of Queen Fortune (the most complete description of her in all of medieval literature, according to Steele) and Venus, and then gathers short poems written to her. The ballades are culled from various points in the Duke's writing career; Steele notes their non-sequential situation in the Champion French edition, and it is clear that they were drawn together to support a new theme, not new compositions created for a new ensemble.

The nature of this third grouping makes it appear like a work in progress; and it is tempting indeed to intuit Charles' *modus operandi* from the creation recorded *in medias res*. Did he actually follow the sequence suggested by the three ensembles: first, invent a narrative framework with setting, characters, and plot; second, review his extant collection of short poems to find those which might fit into a sequence within the narrative frame; third, compose the closing part of the narrative; and fourth, rewrite the whole, strengthening the internal unity which he had already imposed from the exterior, subordinating the parts to the whole. Such a procedure is possible to imagine, given the state of these three ensembles, from the first which is most coherent, most finished, and most neatly constructed, the second which is beginning to take shape, and the third which is only in the early stages of formation. The allegorical mode is most skillfully used in the first (or finished) ensemble; it is not functional in the second, and it occurs in a manner new to Charles' rhetorical repertoire in the third (or least finished) work.

* * *

A review of the longer verse by Charles d'Orléans was undertaken in order to determine the role of the allegorical mode in its most frequent terrain, the sustained narrative, and to assess the differences, if any, between his use of allegorical figures in the short lyric and the extended poem or composite ensemble. Three concepts emerge from this examination: first, that his poetic vision included compositions more ambitious in scope than an occasional rondeau or ballade; second, that he seems to have viewed narrative as a component, not an end in itself; and third, that he was an innovator on a modest scale, not merely a redactor *à forme fixe*.

The longer works are sometimes outstanding within the greater poetic corpus only by virtue of length. In some instances, they show no concept of unity or consciousness of the potentiality afforded by literary time and space. Eventually, Charles seems to have recognized diversity in form and tone as one of the exigencies of expansion; the difference between the *Canticum Amoris* and the Early Ballade Cycle, resulting in the artistic success of the latter and the essential monotony of the former, comes from the deliberate exploitation of variety as a means to complexity or enrichment. Both sequences are somber, but the Early Ballade Cycle is poetically interesting to a degree never attained in the *Canticum Amoris.*

The Duke's concept of the role of narrative may have come from his early training at the hands of scholastics with a particular schema of rhetoric to impart. He considers story-telling as one of many possible techniques, always to be used as a subordinate member, never as a goal in itself. This may also be part of an explanation for the lack of a sustained narrative in allegory, despite a definite preference for allegorical expression.

Finally, it is in the longer ensembles that Charles appears as the innovator, with considerable creativity. True, expanded compositions were being written experimentally throughout the later Middle Ages; the *Divina Commedia,* the *Vita Nuova,* Christine de Pisan's *Cent Ballades,* and the collections of stories (such as the *Canterbury Tales*) are all efforts to construct more elaborate works on a vaster structural plane. Each of these evidences a different kind of inner unity; each depends on separable entities as the minimal unit of structure. Charles d'Orléans too experiments with a combination of short verse *à forme fixe* and rhetorical mortar so that the ballades or rondeaux are illustrations of an announced theme (like the *Vita Nuova*) or are themselves filled with matters of intrigue (like the individual cantos of the *Divina Commedia*), or are reactions to an unannounced plot development, which is to be inferred from the content of the shorter poems (like the *Cent Ballades*). It is in the longer poetic ensembles that Charles' great talent in organization and structuring is most apparent, and his role as a creative artist is most clearly articulated. His use of the allegorical mode varies only slightly when he works in an expanded format; he continues to rely heavily on the named abstraction; and only once attempts a depiction of an active allegorical figure with the accoutrements customarily associated with such portrayals. The result is a less satisfactory long poem designed for a composition he did not finish. It is safe to conclude that the developed allegorical figure so typical of narratives in his era did not interest him.

V

COURTLY METAPHOR AND ALLEGORY

The preceding chapters have tended toward this assertion: in the poetry of the Duke of Orleans, both English and French, personification does exist but allegory fully developed is not present. To reach such a conclusion must be a leisurely and reflective process, and it has involved four distinct components: 1) a brief examination of allegoresis; 2) a careful review of the types of rhetorical technique related to allegory and exhibited by the poet; 3) a close analysis of a conventional figure, assumedly allegorical, within a limited corpus of poems; 4) a thorough reading of the longer, narrative verse most likely to contain allegory. Allegorical figures and personified abstractions function as mere ornament or as the center of imagery in a briefly elaborated metaphor. So rarely are physical attributes, personalia, or possessions given to them that it is fair to conclude that the mnemonic function of allegory is totally ignored by this poet. Narrative, in that it always is subordinated in rhetorical function, does not support the allegorical figures, which are most often simply named.

Cigada and Fox, who reject the name allegory for the principal stylistic manner of Charles d'Orléans, prefer the phrase "courtly metaphor." Limited in time to the late middle ages, courtly metaphor results from the desire to create metaphor (not merely repeat formulaic imagery) within the perimeters of the existing literary tradition. The trope thus is a type of metaphor whose substantive meaning as well as its formal expression is drawn from medieval courtly conventions. Its roots are in the lyric of Provence, and it grows directly through the *Roman de la Rose.* Cast in figurative language and often referring to familiar abstractions without dwelling upon their depiction or involving them in any prolonged action, it is particularly attractive to any poet of the short lyric because of its conciseness and brevity. An understanding of the workings of courtly metaphor in the writings of Charles d'Orléans accounts for the actual absence of allegory in his works as well as the critical insistence that the impression of allegory is there.

Abstractions and near-allegorical usage abound in his writings, as do personation and personification. Owen lists fourteen types of allegorical device, of which nine occur in the Duke's verse: [1]

1. allegorical armor
    CVIII - 1: Portant harnoys rouillé de Nonchaloir
2. allegorical clothing
    XXXII - 6: enveloppé
        En ung cueuvrechief de Plaisance
4. allegorical dwellings
    L - 3: J'enforcis mon chastel tousjours
        Appellé Joyeuse Plaisance
6. allegorical food
    L - 6: Avitaillié l'ay de Confort
7. allegorical medicaments
    CVII - 13: Medecine devez prendre d'oublye
8. allegorical cleansing
    XXXII - 10: Je l'ay souventesfois lavé
        En larmes de Piteux Penser;
9. allegorical documents
    XCV - 9: Quant je lys ou livre de Joie
10. sermons delivered by personifications
    XXXVII - speech by Espoir to poet and heart
12. mirror
    XXXV - 1-4: J'ay ou tresor de ma pensee
        Un mirouer qu'ay acheté.
        Amour, en l'annee passee,
        Le me vendy, de sa bonté.

Three of the five which are not strictly found in Charles' writings could conceivably be represented if the category designated by Owen is expanded slightly.

---

[1] Dorothy Owen, *Piers Plowman* (London: Univ. of London Press, 1912), pp. 90-126.

3. allegorical steeds, to allegorical transportation
   XXVIII - 1: En la nef de Bonne Nouvelle
11. symbolical significance given to church vestments to symbolical significance given to church doctrine or liturgy
   XXIV - 8: Ou purgatoire de Tristesse
   LXIX - 3-4: Et le service pour son ame
   A chanté Penser Doloreux
13. tree of charity to symbolic tree
   LXXX - 3: l'arbre de Plaisance

Yet these images are never expanded into full-blown allegory; rather the reference is limited to one trait or aspect per poem or abstraction, a mere mentioning rather than an elaboration, a sketching rather than a full portrayal.

Dragonetti notes "*l'ornement* ... *métaphorique*" which is another more likely phrase for Charles' rhetoric, and Dragonetti's typological inventory is closer to the Duke's actual technique than are Owen's fourteen devices:

> le vocabulaire féodale ... le cérémonial du service ... amour et fidélité ... le langage féodale de la soumission ... les symboles du "guerredon" ... autres termes empruntés aux institutions féodales ... métaphores religieuses ... métaphores empruntés aux plantes et à la lumière ...[2]

Courtly metaphor draws on the extensive vocabularies of the great medieval institutions, feudalism, church, ritualized love as opposed to full-blown allegory which exists in the external medieval landscape of castles, armor, horses and the other realia of daily life.

In postulating three stages of stylistic development in the Duke's career, Cigada depends heavily on the nature of courtly metaphor and its evidence throughout Charles' art. The early or first phase identified by Cigada "*Metaforizzazione della maniere cortese*" (L'Opera poetica, p. 96) yields to "*Il naturalismo precioso*" which in turn gives way to "*realismo psicologico.*" In all three, metaphor itself is the central consideration:

---

[2] R. Dragonetti, *La Technique poétique des trouvères dans la chanson courtoise* (Bruges: de Tempel, 1960), p. 16.

> Cosi avviene che quella che era stata solo metafora sovrimpressa su un dato culturale preofferto, a poco a poco se ne stacca, si isola, e mentre quello, come meno vivo spiritualmente, decade e scompare, la metafora si afferma nel suo valore de dato esperienziale, naturale, e lentamente trapassa in descrizione realista, arte oggetiva. (p. 124)

It is the transformation or alteration of courtly metaphor that Cigada perceives as the growth of Charles the artist, from England to Blois, and he cites the constant presence of metaphor at all moments in the poet's lifetime.

> ... questa maniera, da un lato amoroso-cortese, dell'altro allegorico-metaforica, generatasi dalla prima opera di Charles, reinfluisce su Charles stesso, e finisce per determinare, in parte, la sua nuova produzione; (p. 131).

Allegory and metaphor are inextricably intertwined, for the former cannot and does not stand alone in Charles' verse; and Cigada balances courtliness with "*allegorico-metaforica.*" How does he depict the relationship between allegory, metaphor, figurative language, and the courtly lyric?

> La poesia di Charles d'Orleans tuttavia, questo e ben chiaro, non consiste nella descrizione lirica di un sentimento individuale; e non consiste neanche nel puro acquiescere al cristallizzato, ritmico gioco cortese. Charles ha accostato a questi primi due un terzo piano d'Immagini, che generano tutto un nuovo gioco di rispondenze, e nelle quali consiste la vera, seppur tenue, poesia della ballata: tutta una piccola costellazione di metafore in cui si traspone il gioco del sentimento: (p. 98).

Courtly game *(gioco cortese)*, lyric description of personal feeling *(descrizione lirica di un sentimento individuale)* are joined by Figures *(Immagini)* which appear to be a small cluster of metaphors conveying the interplay of feeling. These Figures relate to allegory as the shadowy incarnations of feelings, the sentimental or sentient figurations.

> ... in genere, semmai, le metafore peccano per difetto, non per excesso. Nello stesso ambito rientrano le notissime figure allegoriche in cui Charles si compiacque per tutta la sua vita, ma specialmente in questa fase. Si è a torto parlato, generalmente molto male, e più necessario, di Dangier, Cueur, Joyeux Espoir o Amour: che in fondo si rilevano appena appena, como lievi ombre colorate e trasparenti, sulla trama del discorso: non vere allegorie, ma solo leggere figurazioni sentimentali, che formano appunto come il sustrato psicologico di quel piu marcato gioco metaforico in cui in vece si contreta l'arte. (p. 102)

Fox agrees that the Duke's poetic figures are "never wholly exteriorized ... never fully committed" (*Lyric Poetry*, p. 69) but, the British critic explains this dominance of metaphor and figure over articulated allegory by hypothesizing about the poet's attitudes toward life, not art. Charles d'Orléans writes

> ... as though he had never decided between the merits of the physical and mental worlds. (p. 69)

The mode of courtly metaphor is intimately connected with Charles' conception of society and the nature of human relations:

> The modern reader may be left with a sense of disappointment by the majority of these images. Their aim is not to startle, nor to carry the mind along unfamiliar tracks. There is no visual impact in this imagery whose nature is cerebral and concerns essentially the likening of abstract to concrete, rarely of concrete to concrete. The "tenor" of Charles' metaphors is usually an emotion: love, melancholy, joy, boredom, and he has not looked far to find the "vehicle." For Charles the image in no way transgresses its context; it fits into a whole scheme, it belongs, it participates, underpinning the whole structure of the courtly tradition, affirming the essentially conservative nature and outlook of its author. (p. 90)

The poetry of the Duke of Orleans is then based upon the extensive use of courtly metaphor, through a rhetoric closely allied to full allegory. The meaning of this metaphor, for Charles, is rooted in the cerebral (as opposed to the physical), the abstract (as against the concrete), and the socio-moral universe of the fifteenth century court with its concepts of love, right conduct, and its code of values. Within this life-sphere, intellectual and actual, abide the sources of those feelings Charles expresses or hopes to evoke through his lyrics. His practice of metaphor belongs in design and content to the era of courtly love, courtly literature, and the long tradition of the formal lyric whose distant antecedents are found in the Provençal troubadours he read, admired, and emulated.

The courtly constraints upon metaphor affect its existence but not its essence. One role of metaphor in any poem is to achieve a satisfying balance between ambiguity and clarity, in a ceaseless fluctuation between the suggestive and the precise. Courtly metaphor is no exception.

If the major concerns of the Duke of Orleans are abstract and cerebral, they are by nature elusive and less than precise; through the use of courtly metaphor, he is able to give the impression of precision which seemingly concretizes those suggestive and ambiguous items he wishes to convey. This is the true function of metaphor as he uses it; and it is the source of the notion that all his verse is allegory, when it actually is not. Through the use of spacial or temporal vocabulary, he sketches the barest outlines of a familiar structure analogous to the totally intellectual concept which is the real meaning of his poem. The result is a subtle blending of abstract and nearly concrete whereby the vagueness and familiarity of the concretism have occasioned the creative participation of the reader and effected the transfer of content with ease and grace.

One may compare this technique with that of the miniature, the more popular type of graphic art during the fifteenth century. Daniel Poirion has noted the similarities between poetry and miniatures at this time:

> Ainsi se répand le goût du décor, de l'image sensible, du beau spectacle. La poésie, sous cette influence, va devenir une représentation, un jeu scénique, une confrontation de personnages individualisés. Elle s'éloigne du chant et se rapproche de la miniature. Le jeu avec les images cesse de soumettre celles-ci au mouvement profond du cœur, à l'élan de la volonté, à l'élévation de la pensée dans la solennité de la cérémonie. (*Le Poète*, p. 79)

The miniature is striking in its details and preciseness, and the technique of courtly metaphor leads to a similar pseudo clarity, which is actually ambiguous and evocative.

Within this tradition of courtly metaphor, how is Charles d'Orléans to be evaluated as imitator or innovator? His works contain evidence of images and words identical to those of others, sometimes drawn from the great cultural heritage, both contemporaneous and antique, within which he was educated: the figures of mythology, from the *Roman de la Rose,* or from tradition (such as, Old Age). He also develops metaphors upon similar types of personification which other poets had also found productive such as the types classified by Owen (the house, elements of clothing) as well as the interior landscape of the inner voice of heart or eye.

As an innovator, he did commit to paper some new combinations of words, but this is always the least interesting type of poetic innovation. His verses contain new phrases (which more thorough and more broad re-readings within this period may relegate to the commonplace) and an exploitation of the spacial or temporal metaphor as opposed to the personal or human personification.

He must be remembered principally as the perfector of courtly metaphor, not its creator or one who amplified its concepts or components. Through his insistent use of the short lyric and his sense of fine restraint, he honed the courtly metaphor to a keenness and elegance of style which few others could match. Like the Japanese caligrapher, his greatest talent is his ability to express simply, evocatively, in distinct yet suggestive lines, an abstract subject.

VI

CHARLES D'ORLÉANS AND HIS CONTEMPORARIES

The Duke of Orleans was above all a cosmopolitan man, exposed to the intellectual currents of at least three national groups at different stages in his exceedingly long lifetime. As an active reader and avid collector of manuscripts, he encountered most of the influential works of his era, and as a man of enforced leisure, he reflected upon them; furthermore, through the meticulous records of his aristocratic household, it is possible to chronicle with some accuracy not only his social but also his literary interests during the four important stages of his life.[1] He is a logical and inevitable candidate for comparative studies of the pre-Renaissance period in France, England, and Italy.

Standing beside those of his contemporaries, his writings are characterized by the dominance of courtly metaphor, the absence of sustained narrative which is the most fruitful ground for allegory during this period, and the restrained use of personification, accompanied by a penchant for meditative verse dealing in abstractions. He appears to be the perfect heir of the fourteenth century, described by Robertson as possessing five cardinal traits: personified abstractions, techniques of the dream vision, elaborate use of exemplary materials, prevailing tendency toward musical expression, and a passion for abstraction.[2] Charles d'Orléans exhibits all of these to a greater or lesser degree. Robertson

---

[1] The best discussion of the libraries is still: Pierre Champion, *La Librairie de Charles d'Orléans* (Paris: Champion, 1910).

[2] D. W. Robertson, Jr., *A Preface to Chaucer* (Princeton: Princeton Univ. Press, 1962), pp. 234-35.

continues by observing the heavy dependence of fourteenth century French literature on the *Roman de la Rose* (p. 231), and in some ways Charles represents the sublime effort to transpose the *Roman* into the short lyric, both stylistically and atmospherically. Finally, Robertson notes quite accurately the role of "reality" in fourteenth century poetry:

> The function of the verisimilitude is, first of all, to attract attention, and ultimately, to show the validity of the underlying abstractions as they manifest themselves in the life of the times. (p. 247)

It is these three criteria, use of courtly metaphor, reaction to the *Roman de la Rose,* and function of verisimilitude, which constitute the grounds for comparing the Duke of Orleans with his peers.

The poets with whose works his should be contrasted are friends with and to whom he wrote verses, in competitions, or in correspondance, or in the privacy of his own notebooks merely because their poems struck a sympathetic chord in him. Long before the school of Blois and its workshop or seminar atmosphere of camaraderie in easy, polite interchange of writings and ideas, Charles had shown an interest in the poetry of others, and he had developed the habit of copying texts into his own manuscripts. To these poems he would occasionally write a ballade or rondeau in reply. Thus in the Champion edition of his French verse there are almost one hundred poems by other authors. The Duke was always careful to include the name of the poet who had arrested his attention, and Champion uses different type fonts to present these borrowed verses. None of these authors had achieved the fame of his copier; with the exception of Villon, all are graceful but secondary versifiers of lesser rank.

Ballades

Within the anthology of ballades, there are several sets of comparative poems, varying in number from one to a score of items per set. All occur more than halfway through the 135 ballades, and most belong to Charles' mature years or his old age.

In order of complexity, they present a variety of styles, themes, and purposes.

1. CIXa   *Pour la conqueste de Mercy*
   Author   Jacques, bastart de la Tremoille
   (Authorship is indicated in the manuscript or identified by Champion.)

This poem does not have an immediate counterpart or response, but its style, content, and use of courtly metaphor made it appealing to Charles, whose verse it strongly resembles. Perhaps its strongest attraction lay in the refrain *"En la forest de longue Actente"* which was one of the Duke's favorite uses, occurring in both rondeaux and ballades.

2. LXXVII   *Je, qui suis Dieu des amoureux*
   Author   Orlians contre Garencieres
   LXXVIIa   *Cupido, Dieu des amoureux*
   Author   Response de Garencieres

This is an example of a ballade with a matching poem composed specifically in answer. Often the opening lines of such pairs are identical, but in this case, the refrains are similar:

> LXXVII   *Des grans biens de ma seigneurie.*
> LXXVIIa   *Le droit de vostre seigneurie.*

Charles in his ballade takes the voice of the God of Love, summoning all his vassals and retainers to help him take vengeance on Garencieres who seeks *"par ... janglerie"* *"... conquerir // Des grans biens de ma seigneurie."* Garencieres and his heart have pledged themselves to Beauty; furthermore the culprit claims to be suffering though he is neither pale nor thin from lovesickness.

Garencieres replies addressing Cupid, to request that *"Un homme de mauvaise vie,"* *"un enfant malicieux,"* *"le prince de Bien Mentir"* (Charles) be punished for usurping Cupid's power. He has already deceived two women in France and is worse than Lucifer, thereby deserving banishment from the Court of Love.

The content, rhetoric, and imagery of both poems is light and precious. They are clearly occasional verse, pleasing by their air of spontaneity and the mock severity of their tone; their aura of affectation and somewhat excessive refinement makes them period pieces of which they are elegant representatives.

3. CIV   *Bon regime sanitatis*
   Author   Par le Duc d'Orlians
   CIVa   *Du regime quod dedistis*
   Author   Fradet

Champion notes that *"Les deux pièces parodient les ordonnances des médecins sur les excès qu'il convient d'éviter pour un nouveau marié, ce qu'était Fradet"* (Champion, *Poésies, II*, p. 559). In Latin, the short verses show the robust male camaraderie in the Duke's friendships; the content is baldly risqué, and the sense of rhetoric as keen as it would have been in a more elegant love ballade. It is Charles who initiates the exchange, and he does not reply to Fradet.

4. CIII   *Present le notaire d'Amours*
   Author *Obligation* de Vaillant
   CIIIa   *A ceulx qui verront ces presentes*
   Author *Vidimus de la dite obligation* par le duc d'Orlians
   CIIIb   *Intendit. Le nomme Vaillant*
   Author *Intendit de la dite obligation* par Me J. Caillau

Champion annotates this set of three as *"Plaisanterie sur les souffrances amoureuses assimilées aux rigueurs de l'ordre des Franciscains reformés"* (*Poésies*, II, p. 559). He dates them after 1453. This little group is immediately preceded by an introductory ballade on a related theme: the similarities between the rule, devotion, and penances of religion to those *"Des amoureux de l'observance"* whose hearts are *"raviz en transe, // Pour venir par perfection // Au hault Paradis de Plaisance."* Vaillant makes, in formal legalistic terms, a renunciation of *"tous droiz d'Amours, Coustume, loy, condition,"* submitting to new jurisdiction and ceding heart, body, wealth, *"Soubz le seel de vostre vouloir."*

The Duke replies by acknowledging, in legal format and jargon, this *"obligation."* The ballade's success clearly depends on the agility with which Charles manages to use the greatest number of professional words in the most graceful manner within the confinement of three stanzas plus envoi.

Vaillant, using the refrain of his opening poem "*Soubz le seeau de vostre vouloir*," presents his answer or "*Intendit*" to the "*Vidimus*." He promises not to fail and to be of good cheer.

This set too is occasional verse, the somewhat desultory sport of litterati, and its artistic merit or excellence is as self-satisfying and limited as was its intended audience. Given the goal of the poet, his success is obvious. Courtly metaphor dominates the group rhetorically.

5. The Burgundian series concerns the Duke's efforts to establish peace in 1439; not only did he write many ballades to Burgundy (LXXXIII, LXXXIV, LXXXV, LCIII, LCIV) which have no recorded answers, but there are two pairs of query-response in Champion's manuscript:

LXXVII	*Puisque, je suis vostre voison*
Refrain	*S'il en estoit a mon vouloir*
Author	Orlians a Bourgogne
LXXXVIIa	*S'il en estoit a mon vouloir*
Author	*Response* de Bourgogne a Orlians
LXXXVIII	*Pour le haste de mon passage*
Refrain	*De cueur, de corps et de puissance*
Author	Orlians a Bourgogne
LXXXVIIIa	*De cueur, de corps et de puissance*
Author	*Response* de Bourgogne a Orlians

The five examples above represent every type of ballade writing in correspondance to be found in the Champion manuscript, except for the *Concours de Blois*. Verisimilitude is absent, although the imagery of some poems is straightforward and non-figurative. The use of courtly metaphor is frequent, and the influence of the *Roman de la Rose* predictably pervasive where appropriate to the subject. Many of these qualify for the designation "occasional" verse, and the intrusion of courtly metaphor into such writing is effectively supportive of tone.

"*Le Concours de Blois*"

The most famous set of ballades for comparative study is that of the Blois competition, involving two opening lines:

> Je meurs de seuf aupres de la fontaine
> Je n'ay plus soif, tairie est la fontaine

It is valued less for artistry than as an evocation of a milieu, as Professor Goodrich has speculated — "Duke Charles reigned in a new kind of court" (*Charles Duke of Orleans*, p. 280). Like the troubadour associated courts of love, this romantic fiction seems to put on flesh and substance as a result of the eleven poems as primary documentation. The verses themselves have attracted less criticism than they have stimulated colorful description of the happy retirement of a dignified poet-prince whose noble largesse was dispensed to cultivate the muse in his own gracious manor. What precisely did the Blois competition produce, poetically? Table I summarizes the order and authorship, following the Champion edition.

CXXIIIb	Poem 1	no author mentioned by Champion
CXXIIIc	Poem 2	no author mentioned by Champion
CXXIIId	Poem 3	Villon?
CXXIIIe	Poem 4	Villon
CXXIIIf		not related to the series, but in the same hand as the preceding poem
CXXIIIg	Poem 5	anonymous, Champion designates northern by style
CXXIIIh	Poem 6	two authors: Monbeton, Robertet
CXXIIIi	Poem 7	anonymous, Champion designates Burgundian by style
CXXIIIj	Poem 8	Berthault de Villebresme
CXXIIIk	Poem 9	M. J. Caillau
CXXIIIl	Poem 10	Gilles des Ourmes
CXXIIIm	Poem 11	Simonnet Caillau

TABLE I: Blois Competition Poems and Authors after Champion

Champion suggests that the ballades were composed between December 1457 and 1460, but he posits no specific chronology of composition apart from their order of appearance in the manuscript (*Vie de Charles d'Orléans*, p. 653). Almost half of these competition pieces are by unknown authors, and all of them are so alike in technique and content as to be nearly indistinguishable. With few exceptions, the line is the primary unit of phrasing. Personal reference and allusion to events of an inner circle unite with universal humane generalizations in each ballade of the series whose themes include group acceptance, illness, money, grief, grammar, and the mild metaphysics implicit in paradox. The last three conclude with a similar rhetorical device as refrain:

Poem 9: Or jugez donc si je vis plaisanment?
Poem 10: Or regardez et jugiez s'il m'ennuye!
Poem 11: Or regardez se tel homme se joue!

Not one contains even a distant echo of the Ovidian conventions of love, in spite of a promising beginning to Poems 9 and 10:

Je meurs de soif aupres de la fontaine;
Tremblant de froit ou feu des amoureaux;

The subject of distorted perception, life in contradiction to the expected is explored through imagery which is frequently corporal, everyday, common, and even banal. Each poem offers several examples of poetically ordinary lines:

Poem 1: Une heure m'est plus d'une quarantaine
Poem 2: Dix mile onces ne me sont que une drame
Poem 3: Ne vert, ne meur, mon ble mengue en grain
Poem 4: Nu comme ung ver, vestu en president
Poem 5: J'ai tresgrant fain, et si ne puis mengier
Poem 6: J'aime et tiens chier tous ceulx qui me font hayne
Ung peu de chose m'est grant comme la mer
Poem 7: Verbe normal, sans conjugacion
Poem 8: Tremblant de froit en manoir chalereux
Poem 9: Et ce qui plaist a tous ne me plaist mie
Poem 10: Beau temps me plaist, et desire la pluye
Poem 11: Parler sçay bien, et ne puis mon cas dire

Abstraction is singularly absent, though once courtly metaphor is used:

Poem 3: Dueil et plaisir me tiennent en commande; The God of Love, fellowship of the Rose, the persons of history, legend, and Scripture are nowhere to be found (again with one exception — Poem 5: *Par trop coart, hardy comme ung Ogier*). No poem turns the fountain into a metaphor of topography, though for the Duke that technique is common elsewhere. In such an absence of courtly metaphor, the use of commonplace realia might be interpreted as a step in the direction of verisimilitude. The entire set is strikingly concrete and unfigurative as though this means had been chosen deliberately in order to put the theme of man-the-unnatural in bas-relief by relying on a strict framework of natural (*i. e.* earthy) associations and ideas.

Similarity of structure, imagery, and emphasis makes all eleven poems like semi-precious stones in a necklace; each is of slightly different hue and tone, but its value is derived mainly from proximity to or combination with its fellows. It has a certain beauty, even luster, in isolation, but strung beside others into a matched set, it is considerably more interesting to the general public as well as the specialist.

"*Rondeau*" Sets

A comparison of the rondeaux written in groups or correspondance is more complicated than was the case for the ballades because the number of pieces is much greater. Of the 435 rondeaux in the Champion edition, ninety are by other authors, primarily on related themes or with first lines identical to those of Charles. They pepper the Duke's whole production chronologically, with some early verses linked directly to much later ones (*i. e.* XVII by Fredet, XVIII and CCCIII by Charles). There are thirty-six rondeau sets, and only three out of this three dozen do not contain a composition by the Duke himself.

Four groups can well stand rival to the famous *Concours de Blois,* and for a study of allegory and courtly metaphor they are crucial. All are based upon identical first lines:

1) "*En la forest de Longue Actente*" — ten poems, eight authors;
2) "*Jaulier des prisons de Pensee*" — five poems, five authors;
3) "*L'abit le moine ne fait pas*" — four poems, four authors;

4) "*Dedans l'abisme de douleur*"—three poems, three authors; with "*Dedens la maison de Douleur*" — two poems, two authors. Each is based on a human figure or a metaphor of place and will reveal well how communal was the technique of courtly metaphor in Charles' peer group.

"*En la forest de Longue Actente*"

Most of the ten poems making up this set are remarkably similar in content and rhetoric, and all except two rely on courtly metaphor as a major instrument. Several poets posit two conventional figures *je* and *mon cuer* and write of the physical misfortune of the latter in the forest: CXXXIII *j'ay esgare mon cueur;* CXXXIV *Deconfort* has the heart captive in his tent; CCXXVII, CCXXVIII the brigands of *Soussy* have captured the heart. Other abstractions may occur, such as *Fortune* (CXXXIII, CCXXV, CCXXVI), *Espoir* (CXXXI, CXXXIV, CXXXVI) or less commonly *Paine, Ennuy* (CXXXI), *Dueil* (CXXXI, CXXXIV), *Beau Parler* (CXXXIII), *Jeunesse* and *Vieilesse* (CCXXV), or *Rigueur* (CXXXIII, CCXXVIII). They carry negative meaning consistently; *Espoir* is most often the purveyor of false promises, and *Fortune* is the source of torment. This usage is appropriate to the wholly unhappy meaning of the accepted first line.

One poem in the set contains no personifications, no personations, no abstractions whatsoever. Jacques, bastart de la Trimoille, is content to develop the metaphor of the forest, scene of the hunt, with a total absence of beings other than himself. Similar to this peripheral member of the collection is the rondeau by Anthoyne de Lussay, where emotions or stages of life are named but not personified: the poet has had no *joye*, no *bien*, and he awaits *la mort,* expecting *aucun plaisir, nul bien.*

Although Gilles, Fredet, and Charles describe interactions involving persons or personalia (*Deconfort*'s tent, *Soussy*'s brigands, *Dure Rigueur* as a guide), none of the other poets interchange the world of ghostly abstractions and the world of human life. Of these three, Fredet and Charles surpass Gilles in elaborateness and complexity: Fredet reports that thirty brigands are taking his heart to *leur seigneur,* and in his response the Duke of Orleans declares his willingness to deal with *le seigneur* himself. In both cases, the metaphor fills the rondeau. Gilles, by comparison, contains his image to one reference in a single line. Charles d'Orléans is the only member of the group to use personified chronological stages (*Jeunesse* and *Vieillesse*), and he alone gives the attribute of speech to an abstraction *(Vieillesse)*.

What is to be inferred from this examination of a rondeau set? It can safely be concluded that Charles uses abstractions with less restraint thant his peers; he goes a step beyond the mere naming of them or deployment in a single brief image. Though the figures are not fully allegorical with appropriate mnemonic accoutrements, they are considerably more humanized by act and association than those of his colleagues.

"*Jaulier des prisons de Pensee*"

In this series, not only the theme but also the very metaphor to be developed is proscribed, and since it involves a person-noun, it offers each of the six poets the possibility of personification immediately. The Duke of Orleans in the initial rondeau sets forth the courtly metaphor in his own recognizable style: addressing *Soussy*, jailer of his heart, he pleads for a cessation of the brutal prison maltreatment being inflicted upon the prisoner. The medium of direct speech, the human label "jailer," the reception of action — these are his preferred techniques of personifications, made strong through combination.

Four of the subsequent rondeaux have the same opening, and they are followed by two more poems in the same vein thematically. How do the principal personages of Charles' poem fare in the other versions? Though the jailer and jailed are omnipresent, their identity may vary: only Orleans insists on *Soussy* as captor (CCCLXXXIII and CCCLXXXVII); for Thignonville, the abstraction is cited as source of authority superior to the jailer (CCCLXXXV) while Benoist Damien puts the noun into a topographic metaphor, *la tour de Soussy* (CCCLXXXVIII). The heart may be the poet's (CCCLXXXIV, CCCLXXXIX) or a pluralized expression synonymous with prisoners (CCCLXXXV), or omitted altogether (CCCLXXXVI). One rondeau of the group is completely non-figurative; the author Gilles des Ourmes sues for the more humane treatment or release of the jailed *gens de bien*. Most of the authors do not rely on personified abstractions to support their imagery, but they are more attracted by the corporal experiences of prison or the human personnel thereof: *larrons, murtries, fers, une bastonneee, la fosse,* lack of money and food. Only one, H. le Voys, prefers the full courtly metaphor, requesting the jailer to admit *Reconfort* who will bring solace from the eyes to the heart held *Ou cep d'Annuy.* Up to this point, the set is not particularly remarkable: given a subject and opening line lending themselves to personification as the primary vehicle of rhetoric, Charles and his associates do not respond to the opportunity with total uniformity. In fact, the contrary is true — courtly metaphor is, for the most part, put aside in favor of verisimilitude.

It is possible that the Duke of Orleans saw in the verses by others the possibilities of a poem based wholly on the concrete (as opposed to the abstract) through the use of vocabulary of the prison milieu and lower class, for the poem immediately following the series (CCXC) is an exercise in personification in the most real and human terms. In a condemnation of *Soussy,* the abstraction is called *ribault, crocheteur,* and *larron.* The poet wishes harsh physical punishment on *Soussy* (I-2 *Battu de verges par la ville,* II-1 *copper une oreille*); he also curses the abstraction in no uncertain terms (III-3 *Le Deable l'ait ou trou Sebille!*). All imagery is physical in origin and un-elevated. The tone is violent and base, non-courtly and unrefined. Here the abstraction serves as a point of departure for non-figurative imagery of a graphic nature. The existence of this poem beside poetry containing the courtly metaphor more common to the Duke's works indicates that he did not abjure more lusty and earthy phrasings through inability, but rather out of choice. He has not left abstractions behind completely in favor of humanity, but he shows an interest in verisimilitude as an aesthetic possibility worthy of exploration.

"*L'abit le moine ne fait pas*"

The proverb poem was one of the more popular types of occasional verse during this period (witness Villon's *Ballade a tout propos* composed totally of aphorisms, sayings and proverbs). This four part set concerns the age-old theme of appearance and its relation to the reality it may conceal. The poets readily turn to personal anecdote or description or to more lofty generalizations in turn. For Jehan Monseigneur de Lorraine this is an opportunity to confess his acceptance of the reverses or pleasures of love, since he only feigns *Douleurs,* while Madame d'Orléans prefers to illustrate the opening line from her own activities — dancing when sad, weeping; and Guiot de Pot chooses to comment on dress and the changes of *Fortune.* The Monseigneur de Lorraine uses the courtly metaphor as the primary device of his poem (CXXV):

> II 1 Je fains d'assembler a grans tas
> Douleurs
> III 2 De nulle rien je ne me dueil
> En gre prens d'Amours le recueil,
> Soit beau ou lait;

In contrast, the other authors exhibit a penchant for the commonplace events and acts of daily life; Charles' contribution is noteworthy for the absence of abstractions though he discusses abstract concepts.

CXXVI

> L'abit le moyne ne fait pas,
> L'ouvrier se congnoist a l'ouvrage
> Et plaisant maintien de visage
> Ne monstre pas toujours le cas.
>
> Aler tout soubrement le pas,
> N'est que contrefaire le sage;
> L'abit le moine [ne fait pas,
> L'ouvrier se congnoist a l'ouvrage.]
>
> Soubtil sens couchie par compas
> Enveloppe en beau langage,
> Musse le vouloir du courage;
> Cuidier deçoit en mains estas;
> L'abit le moine [ne fait pas.]

The first two stanzas are dominated by person-nouns *(le moyne, l'ouvrier, le sage)* or human traits *(visage, pas)* while the last strophe is given to intellectual concerns *(Soubtil sens, le vouloir, courage, cuidier).* Here he contrasts the external and internal worlds without resorting to personifications, courtly conventions, or metaphor. The rhetoric he so frequently employs is an *abit* he can assume or discard at will.

Between the first two poems of the set by the Monseigneur and the Duke intervene two proverb poems by the same authors on a different proverb — "*De fol juge brefve sentence.*" Again the Monseigneur relies on courtly metaphor (CXXVII):

> II 1 La ou Raison pert pascience,
> On voit bien souvent avenir
> De vol juge [briefve sentence.]
> III 1 Envie, atout sa double lance,
> Blesse en mains lieux sans cop ferir,

Charles devotes the first two stanzas to similar rhetoric but turns to non-figurative writing for the concluding strophe.

CXXVIII

> De fol juge brefve sentence;
> On n'y saroit remedyer
> Quant l'advocat Oultrecuidyer,
> Sans raison, maintesfoiz sentence.
>
> Apres s'en repent et s'en tence:
> C'est tart, et ne se puet widyer.
> De fol juge [brefve sentence.]
>
> Fleurs portent odeur; et sentence
> Et savoir vient d'estudyer;
> Ce n'est ne d'annuyt ne d'yer.
> J'en dy ce que mon cuer sent en ce:
> De fol juge brefve sentence.

The *cuer* is a way of saying "intuition" here, not the courtly conventional heart interacting with the eyes in the complicated ritual of Love.

From this rondeau set it can be seen that a mixture of courtly metaphor and the preoccupation with daily event that is a prerequisite for verisimilitude occur with equal frequency in the writings by the Duke of Orleans and his circle. It is impossible to conclude that one technique gave way to another but the coexistence of both modes contradicts the cliche of Orléans the allegorist.

"*Dedens l'abisme de douleur, Dedens la maison de Douleur*"
(CXXXIX, CXL, CXLI; CCCCXXII, CCCCXIII)

In actuality there are two small sets here, each of which is a unit and completely distinctive; they illustrate well the possibilities afforded by such an opening line for the use of courtly metaphor or not, at the will of the poet. The earlier three poems are striking similar in content. The Duke of Orleans and Cadet d'Alebret address ladies or an individual lady respectively to solicit mercy or release of the souls of lovers of the swains' heart, and Gilles des Ormes laments the suffering of "*Maints cuers*" as a result of the capricious cruelty of those whom they have served. The role of lover is filled by *cueur*, also called *bon serviteur*, the *ames Des amans* or *Maints cuers*, a singularly uniform mode of reference. Charles and Gilles des Ormes include an abstraction in the form of *Dangier* (CXL) and *Pitie* (CXLI) with an apostrophizing adjective phrase or projected behavior as the means of personification. Courtly metaphor does not occur in the first three poems or set beyond the topography of the opening line which functions as setting for the entire poem in each of the three cases: the *cuer*, the *ames*, and the *cuers* are all in this dreadful abyss, and the rondeau is both a description of their sad situation and an appeal for aid.

The second set, based on a topographic metaphor unusually close to the wording of the first group, turns out to be quite dissimilar. The Duke's poem is unlike his earlier rondeau and shows his ability to arrive at a different style even while starting from the same point of origin. He tells how *Soussy, Viellesse, Desplaisance* dance to the drummer *Maleur* and the songs of *Pleur* in the house of *Doleur* where the poet falls asleep of *ennuy*. The entire imagery of the poem is dependent on courtly metaphor, and the poet's meaning is conveyed exclusively through the mechanics of personified or concretized abstractions. Unlike CXL where the poet pleaded with *Mes Dames* in collectivity for the succor of the *ames Des amans* under the threat of *Dangier*, all vague and general, here he sketches a scene through individual or precise abstractions each one of which sustains or elaborates the image in metaphor.

The second contributor to the small group, Simmonet Caillau, describes with the vocabulary of illness and the sickroom the heart lying on the *"piteulx lit de Pleur."* His rondeau too relies on courtly metaphor but not so extensively as that by the Duke of Orleans.

These five poems, two of which are by Charles, demonstrate that he and his peers drew on courtly metaphor in varying degrees; it is not a chronologically or personally limitable phenomenon.

After reviewing four rondeau sets and the Blois competition series it is possible to see that courtly metaphor wa a common component of the working *ars rhetorica* in Charles' peer group. Yet he alone seems to have grasped the full potential of the device, exploring the peripheral areas of its perimeters of function most fearlessly and knowingly. It appears to have attracted and rewarded him more fully than the others, although not every poem he composed contains evidence of his mastery of courtly metaphor.

He ventures in the direction of verisimilitude, and he uses the type of figure associated with the *Roman de la Rose* though he never combines the two techniques. His practice of courtly metaphor may have restrained any greater drive toward verisimilitude while forcing a continuation of the traditional references to or naming of familia Roseate abstractions. He is a conservative artist, settled comfortably among his friends and in his times, with a predilection for courtly metaphor that simultaneously supports his group affiliation while setting him apart from his fellows.

VII

CONCLUSION

Charles as Allegorist

Charles d'Orléans has long held the reputation of allegorist, an impression supported by the occurrence of abstract nouns and the naming of allegorical figures throughout his writings. At the outset of this study, critical horror of allegory appeared to constitute a major stumbling block to an appreciation and positive evaluation of his poetry. An analysis of the workings of rhetoric in the short lyrics which make up the bulk of his work and in the rare narratives and longer poems he composed reveals that he wrote in the allegorical mode, but did he write allegory itself?

Charles' writing is characterized by five salient traits:

1. lack of mnemonic detail or portrayal of personified abstractions.
2. lack of sustained, complicated plot.
3. use of narrative as a minor rather than major component.
4. presence of named personifications, persons, and conventional intermediate beings (heart, eyes).
5. frequent occurrence of phrasal metaphors, based upon abstract nouns, as the primary rhetorical tool.

These characteristics contradict the existing definitions of allegoresis, wholly or in part. Therefore, what might have seemed to be full allegory is actually the allegorical mode, pseudo-allegory, or allegory-like writing. Every critic of allegory insists upon duality of meaning as the essential criterion of judgment. In the poetry of Charles d'Orléans where the crucial element is the metaphor, frequently only a phrase, the double levels of meaning potentially viable within the metaphor are present. Often, however, the success of the poem depends not on the preservation of two levels of meaning, but on their merger into one simple message; yet another canon of allegory is thereby violated.

The five traits of Charles' work are intrinsic to the short lyric, an artistic endeavor different, *sui generis,* from the sustained narrative. Plot, portrayal, chronicle cannot be developed within the limited space of the *ballade, chanson* or *rondeau,* and metaphor is ideally suited to this medium where brevity and conciseness are fundamental. Although dual levels of meaning, intrigue, and fully depicted abstractions can be presented in small works (the cameo appearances within larger narratives are often strikingly successful), full allegory is unlikely in the short poem. Metaphors may be similar to, or reminiscent of allegory, but metaphor is not allegory.[1]

Continuity and Innovation

Charles d'Orléans stands on the threshhold of the Renaissance. Given the finest medieval education his family and the Sorbonne could provide, he was also open to all of those currents of change, Italian, English, and French, that would be recognized later as formative and crucial for western Europe's intellectual rebirth. He inherited a fine library to which he made steady additions throughout a lifetime during which his social status and condition offered him leisure to study, to reflect, and to compose. Through travel, through an extended period in a foreign culture, through his own interest in *belles lettres,* and by chronological accident, he not only lived in a time of upheaval and renewal, but he had every opportunity to lead or explore the avenues of the future of literature. In what ways did he reject the medieval and move toward the new techniques, themes, and ideas?

Rhetorically, the new era would be liberated from the dominance of allegory. It would also claim the narrative as a primary

---

[1] Is this distinction yet another petty semantic point? To the fifteenth-century poet, the intricacies of rhetoric were more commonplace than they may be to the twentieth-century reader. The formal poet deserves our scrupulous attention to the practices he valued.

form rather than a trope among many others. And it would depend upon new forms for the lyric. In that Charles did not succumb to the temptations of full allegory, he is set apart from the late medieval period, but his replacement (courtly metaphor) is not new in the fifteenth century. None of his preferred rhetoric can be called novel at the time when he creates. He does not invent new modes, but rather claims a device with certain attendant and dependent subjects or themes, to be placed in the short lyric to which they are most suited, and rises to new heights of artistry in their use. In that his preferred form was already in existence when he wrote and in his rhetorical closeness to his predecessors (Christine de Pisan, the early Chaucer, and Petrarch), he is not innovative.

Yet, while in England, he did venture into spheres of poetry new to him and potentially leading into fresh by-ways. He experiments in the kaleidoscopic ensemble of small structural units, as did many of his late-medieval peers, he composes some original ensembles, based upon new concepts of unity and variety, He attempts at least one narrative, unsuccessfully, but he does not transport the English modes, with which he flirted, to the soil of France when his exile ends in 1441.

The themes and ideas he expresses are also not new, and as they are linked to the forms within which they are stated, perhaps their lack of novelty is not surprising. Still, feudalism, love's service within the courtly framework, and the activities or pastimes of the aristocracy are not the matter of which the Renaissance masters will make poems, any more than they will prefer the *ballade* or *rondeau*.

Lebovics sees Charles as a man who rejected the medieval:

> Thus Charles lends support to the Huizinga thesis that the fifteenth century is an age of an autumnal civilization. Contrary to Huizinga's theory, however, Charles does not cling desperately to the outworn values of a dying age. For Charles, it is a time for the breaking of values. His naivete masks a cynical sophistication; his easy laughter reveals a world barren of meaning.
> The lightness and triviality of his verse, which so enraged the nineteenth century, was the only possible response of a man who had outgrown all the cherished beliefs of

his civilization; who finds nothing to take seriously because, for him, there is nothing.[2]

An examination of the use of courtly metaphor and the allegorical mode in the writings of the Duke of Orleans does not support her thesis. He did not reject, but rather selected and refined from the medieval tradition to which he belonged by inclination and choice.

His concept of man and literature is courtly, aristocratic, and essentially medieval. His poetry is dominated by courtly metaphor, rhetorical virtuosity, shows little thematic variety, and is preoccupied with courtly love, mystical religiosity, and a certain social milieu. He read and discarded Chaucer's *Canterbury Tales* and Petrarch's sonnets, and did not know of or rejected the *Divina Commedia* and the *Decamerone*. Through an analysis of rhetoric in his works and through comparisons with his contemporaries, his deeply conservative nature emerges most clearly, and he can be seen as a fifteenth century man of ideas who consciously chose to exercise his talents through the established order and tradition of his times.

---

[2] Victoria Lebovics, "The Moral Universe of Charles d'Orléans," (Diss. Yale 1962), p. 281.

SELECTED BIBLIOGRAPHY

Beaufils, Constant. *Etude sur la vie et les poésies de Charles d'Orléans.* Coutances: Imp. Salettes, 1861.

Champion, Pierre. "Du Succès de l'œuvre de Charles d'Orléans et de ses imitateurs jusqu'au XVIᵉ siècle." *Mélanges offerts à M. E. Picot,* Vol. I. Paris: D. Morgand, 1913, pp. 409-420.

Champion, Pierre. *Histoire poétique du quinzième siècle,* I. Paris: Champion, 1923.

Champion, Pierre. *La Librairie de Charles d'Orléans.* Paris: Champion, 1910.

Champion, Pierre. *Vie de Charles d'Orléans.* Paris: Champion, 1923.

Champillion-Figeac, A. *Louis et Charles, ducs d'Orléans, leur influences sur les arts, la littérature et l'esprit de leur siècle.* Paris: 1844.

Charles d'Orléans, *Poésies.* Ed. Pierre Champion. 1923, rpt. Paris: Champion, 1966.

Charpier, Jacques. *Vie et œuvres de Charles d'Orléans.* Ecrivains d'hier et d'aujourd'hui. Paris: Pierre Seghers, 1958.

Choffel, Jacques. *Le Duc Charles d'Orléans.* Paris: Debresse, 1968.

Christine de Pisan, *Ballades, Rondeaux, and Virelais.* Ed. Kenneth Varty. Leicester: Leicester Univ. Press, 1965.

Cigada, Sergio. "Christine de Pisan e la tradizione inglese delle poesie di Charles d'Orléans." *Aevum,* 32 (1958), 509-516,

Cigada, Sergio. *L'Opera poetica di Charles d'Orleans.* Milan: Società Editrice Vita e Pensiero, 1960.

Coleridge, S. T. *Miscellaneous Criticism.* Ed. T. M. Raysor. Cambridge: Harvard Univ. Press, 1936.

Curtius, Ernst Robert. *European Literature and the Latin Middle Ages.* Trans. Willard R. Trask. 1953: rpt. New York: Harper, 1963.

Dragonetti, R. *La Technique poétique des trouvères dans la chanson courtoise.* Bruges: de Tempel, 1960.

Fletcher, Angus. *Allegory.* Ithaca: Cornell Univ. Press, 1964.

Fox, John. *The Lyric Poetry of Charles d'Orléans.* Cambridge: Cambridge Univ. Press, 1969.

Glauser, Alfred. *Le Poème-symbole.* Paris: Nizet, 1967.

Goodrich, Norma Lorre *Charles Duke of Orleans: A Literary Biography.* New York: Macmillan, 1963.

Goodrich, Norma Lorre. *Charles of Orleans: A Study of Themes in His French and in His English Poetry.* Geneva: Droz, 1967.

Guiette, Robert. "D'une Poésie formelle en France au moyen âge." *Questions de littérature*. Gent: Romanica Gandensia, 1960.
Haskins, Charles Homer. *The Renaissance of the Twelfth Century*. 1927; rpt. New York: Meridian Books, 1961.
Hauser, Arnold. *Mannerism*. London: Routledge and Kegan Paul, 1965.
Héricault, Charles Joseph de Ricault (also called d'Héricault). *Poésies complètes de Charles d'Orléans*, I. Paris: Flammarion, 1874.
Huizinga, Johan. *The Waning of the Middle Ages*. 1924; rpt. New York: Doubleday, 1949.
Jeanroy, Alfred. *Les Origines de la poésie lyrique en France au moyen âge*. Paris: Champion, 1925.
Julleville, Petit de. *Histoire de la langue et de la littérature française*, I. Paris: Colin, 1896.
Kühl, Ferdinand. *Die Allegorie bei Charles d'Orléans*. Marburg, 1886.
Lebovics, Victoria. "The Moral Universe of Charles d'Orléans." Diss. Yale, 1962.
Lewis, C. S. *The Allegory of Love*. 1936; rpt. New York: Oxford Univ. Press, 1958.
MacLeod, Enid. *Charles of Orleans: Prince and Poet*. New York: Viking, 1969.
Montgomery, Robert L., Jr. "Allegory and the Incredible Fable: The Italian View from Dante to Tasso." *PMLA*, 81 (1966), pp. 45-55.
Ouy, Gilbert. *Un poème mystique de Charles d'Orléans, le Canticum Amoris*. Milan: Società Editrice Internazionale, 1959.
Owen, Dorothy L. *Piers Plowman: A Comparison with Some Earlier and Contemporary French Allegories*. London: Hodder and Stoughton, 1912.
Albert Pauphilet, ed. *Poètes et romanicers du moyen âge*. Bibliothèque de la Pléiade. Paris: Gallimard, 1952.
Poirion, Daniel. "Création poétique et composition romanesque de Charles d'Orléans." *Revue des sciences humaines*, April-June 1958, pp. 185-211.
Poirion, Daniel. *Le Lexique de Charles d'Orléans dans les Ballades*. Geneva: Droz, 1967.
Poirion, Daniel. *Le poète et le prince*. Paris: Presses Universitaires de France, 1965.
Robertson, D. W., Jr. *A Preface to Chaucer*. Princeton: Princeton Univ. Press, 1962.
Siciliano, Italo. *François Villon et les thèmes poétiques du moyen âge*. Paris: Colin, 1934.
Skeat, Walter W. *Chaucer Complete Works*. 1912; rpt. London: Oxford Univ. Press, 1965.
Spenser, Edmund. *The Faerie Queene*. Ed. Robert Kellogg and Oliver Steele. New York: Odyssey, 1965.
Steele, Robert. *The English Poems of Charles of Orleans*. Early English Text Society, Series 215. Oxford: Oxford Univ. Press, 1941.
Steele, Robert, and Mabel Day. *The English Poems of Charles of Orleans*. Early English Text Society, Series 220. Oxford: Oxford Univ. Press, 1946.
Villon, François. *Poésies choisies*. Ed. J. Passeron. Paris: Larousse, 1960.

Williams, Arnold. "Medieval Allegory: An Operational Approach." *Poetic Theory/Poetic Practice, Papers of the Midwest Modern Language Association*, I (1969), pp. 77-84.

Zumthor, Paul. "Charles d'Orléans et le langage de l'allégorie." *Mélanges offerts à Rita Lejeune, Professeur à l'Université de Liège*. Ed. J. Duculot. Gembloux, 1968.

NORTH CAROLINA STUDIES IN THE ROMANCE LANGUAGES AND LITERATURES

I.S.B.N. Prefix 0-88438

Recent Titles

THE OLD PORTUGUESE "VIDA DE SAM BERNARDO," EDITED FROM ALCOBAÇA MANUSCRIPT CCXCI/200, WITH INTRODUCTION, LINGUISTIC STUDY, NOTES, TABLE OF PROPER NAMES, AND GLOSSARY, by Lawrence A. Sharpe. 1971. (No. 103). *-903-0.*

A CRITICAL AND ANNOTATED EDITION OF LOPE DE VEGA'S "LAS ALMENAS DE TORO," by Thomas E. Case. 1971. (No. 104). *-904-9.*

LOPE DE VEGA'S "LO QUE PASA EN UNA TARDE," A CRITICAL, ANNOTATED EDITION OF THE AUTOGRAPH MANUSCRIPT, by Richard Angelo Picerno. 1971. (No. 105). *-905-7.*

OBJECTIVE METHODS FOR TESTING AUTHENTICITY AND THE STUDY OF TEN DOUBTFUL "COMEDIAS" ATTRIBUTED TO LOPE DE VEGA, by Fred M. Clark. 1971. (No. 106). *-906-5.*

THE ITALIAN VERB. A MORPHOLOGICAL STUDY, by Frede Jensen. 1971. (No. 107). *-907-3.*

A CRITICAL EDITION OF THE OLD PROVENÇAL EPIC "DAUREL ET BETON," WITH NOTES AND PROLEGOMENA, by Arthur S. Kimmel. 1971. (No. 108). *-908-1.*

FRANCISCO RODRIGUES LOBO: DIALOGUE AND COURTLY LORE IN RENAISSANCE PORTUGAL, by Richard A. Preto-Rodas. 1971. (No. 109). *-909-X.*

RAIMOND VIDAL: POETRY AND PROSE, edited by W. H. W. Field. 1971. (No. 110). *-910-3.*

RELIGIOUS ELEMENTS IN THE SECULAR LYRICS OF THE TROUBADOURS, by Raymond Gay-Crosier. 1971. (No. 111). *-911-1.*

THE SIGNIFICANCE OF DIDEROT'S "ESSAI SUR LE MERITE ET LA VERTU," by Gordon B. Walters. 1971. (No. 112). *-912-X.*

PROPER NAMES IN THE LYRICS OF THE TROUBADOURS, by Frank M. Chambers. 1971. (No. 113). *-913-8.*

STUDIES IN HONOR OF MARIO A. PEI, edited by John Fisher and Paul A. Gaeng. 1971. (No. 114). *-914-6.*

DON MANUEL CAÑETE, CRONISTA LITERARIO DEL ROMANTICISMO Y DEL POSROMANTICISMO EN ESPAÑA, por Donald Allen Randolph. 1972. (No. 115). *-915-4.*

THE TEACHINGS OF SAINT LOUIS. A CRITICAL TEXT, by David O'Connell. 1972. (No. 116). *-916-2.*

HIGHER, HIDDEN ORDER: DESIGN AND MEANING IN THE ODES OF MALHERBE, by David Lee Rubin. 1972. (No. 117). *-917-0.*

JEAN DE LE MOTE "LE PARFAIT DU PAON," édition critique par Richard J. Carey. 1972. (No. 118). *-918-9.*

CAMUS' HELLENIC SOURCES, by Paul Archambault. 1972. (No. 119). *-919-7.*

FROM VULGAR LATIN TO OLD PROVENÇAL, by Frede Jensen. 1972. (No. 120). *-920-0.*

GOLDEN AGE DRAMA IN SPAIN: GENERAL CONSIDERATION AND UNUSUAL FEATURES, by Sturgis E. Leavitt. 1972. (No. 121). *-921-9.*

THE LEGEND OF THE "SIETE INFANTES DE LARA" (*Refundición toledana de la crónica de 1344* versión), study and edition by Thomas A. Lathrop. 1972. (No. 122). *-922-7.*

STRUCTURE AND IDEOLOGY IN BOIARDO'S "ORLANDO INNAMORATO," by Andrea di Tommaso. 1972. (No. 123). *-923-5.*

STUDIES IN HONOR OF ALFRED G. ENGSTROM. edited by Robert T. Cargo and Emanuel J. Mickel, Jr. 1972. (No. 124). *-924-3.*

A CRITICAL EDITION WITH INTRODUCTION AND NOTES OF GIL VICENTE'S "FLORESTA DE ENGANOS," by Constantine Christopher Stathatos. 1972. (No. 125). *-925-1.*

Recent Titles

LI ROMANS DE WITASSE LE MOINE. *Roman du treizième siècle*. Édité d'après le manuscrit, fonds français 1553, de la Bibliothèque Nationale, Paris, par Denis Joseph Conlon. 1972. (No. 126). *-926-X.*

EL CRONISTA PEDRO DE ESCAVIAS. *Una vida del Siglo XV*, por Juan Bautista Avalle-Arce. 1972. (No. 127). *-927-8.*

AN EDITION OF THE FIRST ITALIAN TRANSLATION OF THE "CELESTINA," by Kathleen V. Kish. 1973. (No. 128). *-928-6.*

MOLIÈRE MOCKED. THREE CONTEMPORARY HOSTILE COMEDIES: *Zélinde, Le portrait du peintre, Élomire Hypocondre*, by Frederick Wright Vogler. 1973. (No. 129). *-929-4.*

C.-A. SAINTE-BEUVE. *Chateaubriand et son groupe littéraire sous l'empire*. Index alphabétique et analytique établi par Lorin A. Uffenbeck. 1973. (No. 130). *-930-8.*

THE ORIGINS OF THE BAROQUE CONCEPT OF "PEREGRINATIO," by Juergen Hahn. 1973. (No. 131). *-931-6.*

THE "AUTO SACRAMENTAL" AND THE PARABLE IN SPANISH GOLDEN AGE LITERATURE, by Donald Thaddeus Dietz. 1973. (No. 132). *-932-4.*

FRANCISCO DE OSUNA AND THE SPIRIT OF THE LETTER, by Laura Calvert. 1973. (No. 133). *-933-2.*

ITINERARIO DI AMORE: DIALETTICA DI AMORE E MORTE NELLA "VITA NUOVA," by Margherita de Bonfils Templer. 1974. (No. 134). *-934-0.*

L'IMAGINATION POETIQUE CHEZ DU BARTAS; ELEMENTS DE SENSIBILITE BAROQUE DANS LA "CREATION DU MONDE," by Bruno Braunrot. 1974. (No. 135). *-935-9.*

ARTUS DESIRE, PRIEST AND PAMPHLETEER OF THE SIXTEENTH CENTURY, by Frank Giese. 1974. (No. 136). *-936-7.*

"JARDIN DE NOBLES DONZELLAS" BY FRAY MARTÍN DE CÓRDOBA, by Harriet Goldberg. 1974. (No. 137). *-937-5.*

VISUAL VARIETY AND SPATIAL GRANDEUR: A STUDY OF THE TRANSITION FROM THE SIXTEENTH TO THE SEVENTEENTH FRENCH CENTURY, by John F. Winter. 1974. (No. 140). *-940-5.*

Essays

MOLIERE: TRADITIONS IN CRITICISM, by Laurence Romero. 1974. (Essays, No. 1). *-001-7.*

STUDIES IN TIRSO, I, by Ruth Lee Kennedy. 1974. (Essays, no. 3), *-003-3.*

Texts, Textual Studies and Translations

LAS MEMORIAS DE GONZALO FERNÁNDEZ DE OVIEDO, Vols. I and II, by Juan Bautista Avalle-Arce. 1974. (Texts, Textual Studies, and Translations, Nos 1 and 2). *-401-2; 402-0.*

Symposia

ESTUDIOS DE LITERATURA HISPANOAMERICANA EN HONOR A JOSÉ J. ARROM, edited by Andreñ P. Debicki and Enrique Pupo-Walker. 1975. (Symposia, No. 2). *952-9.*

When ordering please cite the *ISBN Prefix* plus the last four digits for each title.
Send orders to:

      International Scholarly Book Service, Inc.
      P.O. Box 4347
      Portland, Oregon 97208
      U.S.A.